Finding Emotional Wellness After a Narcissistic Relationship

Never Again. Explore The Reasons You Attract Narcissistic Personalities and Learn to Protect Yourself from Emotional Manipulation

Table of Contents

INTRODUCTION 5

CHAPTER 1 - UNRAVELING NARCISSISM 11

THE 7 WARNING SIGNS OF NARCISSISTIC PERSONALITY DISORDER .. 11
WHAT CAUSES NARCISSISM? 17
4 TYPES OF NARCISSISTS YOU NEED TO STAY AWAY FROM 19
THE 4 TYPES OF PEOPLE THAT NARCISSISTS ARE ATTRACTED TO 21

CHAPTER 2 - STAYING ONE STEP AHEAD 24

11 WAYS TO KNOW YOU'RE IN A RELATIONSHIP WITH A NARCISSIST 24
DANGEROUS MANIPULATION TACTICS USED BY NARCISSISTS 31
5 THINGS EVERY NARCISSIST LIKES TO SAY 38
5 TRIGGERS FOR NARCISSISTIC RAGE 40

CHAPTER 3 - WHEN ENOUGH IS ENOUGH 46

5 ESSENTIAL TIPS FOR DEALING WITH A NARCISSIST THE RIGHT WAY 46
5 PHRASES TO INSTANTLY DISARM A NARCISSIST 51

CHAPTER 4 - CUTTING THE CORD 56

WHY IT'S SO HARD TO BREAK UP WITH A NARCISSIST 56
THE 7 STAGES OF TRAUMA BONDING 58
HOW TO BREAK UP WITH A NARCISSIST FOR GOOD 59
USING THE GRAY ROCK METHOD TO YOUR ADVANTAGE 62

CHAPTER 5 - HEALING FROM NARCISSISTIC ABUSE 65

THE 5 STAGES OF RECOVERY FROM NARCISSISTIC ABUSE 66

5 Transformative Truths Every Victim Must Face 70
Essential Exercises to Strengthen the Healing Heart & Mind 75
Life-Altering Affirmations to Heal Past Hurts 78

CHAPTER 6 - BREAKING THE CYCLE 82

6 Reasons Why You Keep Attracting Narcissists 82
7 Ways to Spot a Narcissist on the First Date 86
4 Ways to Stop Attracting Narcissists Once and for All 90
9 Powerful Tips for Developing Unbreakable Self-Love 93

CHAPTER 7 - LOVING AGAIN 98

7 Mistakes to Avoid When You Start Dating Again 98
5 Early Signs You've Finally Found a Good Partner 103
8 Great Habits to Start Your New Relationship the Right Way 106

CONCLUSION 111

Introduction

If you've picked up this book, you may be wondering if you're in a relationship with a narcissist. Alternatively, you may know you're in a relationship with a narcissist and are now wondering how to get out of it. Or you might be trying to assess if you really need to get out or if things will get better.

Our you may have come to this book because you have come out of a relationship that started off well but then left you so bruised and unsure of what went wrong that you are now looking for ways to heal and move on. You want to avoid a repeat of the devastation that a narcissist can wreak on your wellbeing.

Some of you may even be in a new relationship with someone who was hurt by a narcissist and wants to know how to help them move forward.

Whatever brought you here, you've come to the right place. In the chapters that follow, you'll learn how to identify narcissistic abuse and how to spot a narcissist, so you don't get stung again. You'll learn what they say, what they do, and how they react.

You'll learn how to protect yourself and use techniques to back away so that you don't attract the rage of this particularly difficult personality type. Most importantly, you'll be given the tools to help you recover from your experience and move on with your life to a happier future and better relationships.

As someone who has come across a few narcissists in my time, I have closely studied this troubling personality type and unlocked many of the secrets that make them who they are. Once you truly understand them, they lose their hold over you and reveal themselves for what they are — troubled and deeply lonely individuals who are sadly too damaged to enjoy healthy, balanced relationships with others. *You* can't help them.

Read this book, and you'll come away not only with greater understanding but also the tools to free yourself of the narcissist in your life. You can look forward to greater peace and security in your future relationships, a sense of safety and wellbeing, and greater self-confidence — something that a narcissist is quite skilled at undermining.

Here's what we'll cover:

- **How to spot a narcissist**

You'll find out what they'll say to you, how they will get under your skin and, most importantly, how they'll make you feel. We'll look at the different types of narcissists and some examples of how they tend to behave in certain situations, for example, on a first date.

We'll also look at what makes someone into a narcissist, and who they really are under that tough exterior (clue: very immature). Knowing just how small and frightened these people are beneath that smooth surface is key to understanding their behavior and to no longer being affected by it.

- **How to recover from narcissistic abuse**

A narcissist can do damage seemingly without regret. With their words and their behavior, they can have you doubting yourself, feeling unsure of your sanity, and living in a state of siege. They thrive on drama, discord, and conflict, while the people around them struggle to do anything apart from ward off their next attack. But you can break this cycle and not fall into it again.

In this book, you'll find out how to empower yourself, heal, and restore your sense of self-worth after narcissistic abuse. We'll also look at how to safely break up, disengage or move on from a narcissist without attracting their narcissistic rage.

- **How to deal with a narcissist in the moment**

Unfortunately, this personality trait is reasonably common. In fact, there are times when it's easier to simply get along with a narcissist. One example is when you have one at your workplace and you otherwise love your job. Another is when you have a narcissistic family member who you have to maintain some contact with for the sake of the wider peace. Why should you leave to escape just this one person?

The answer is, you don't. But what you do need are some simple techniques to prepare for those encounters. This way, you can deal with the narcissist in a calm, assertive manner "in the moment" when they attempt to push your buttons. The other benefit of this is that they are likely to get bored, move on to their next victim, and leave you alone.

- **How to escape from a narcissist**

One thing that narcissists cannot tolerate is being ignored or abandoned. This triggers all of their buried feelings, often buried from childhood, that led them to behave abusively in the first place. You can be certain that they will make leaving as difficult for you as it is for them. Once you have escaped, the narcissist in your life will simply move on to someone else — but before that happens, you can expect an escalation of all of their worst behaviors. In the most serious cases, you may be in actual danger.

However, there are ways to disarm the narcissist, back away slowly, and protect yourself. These can be learned. Most importantly, these techniques will make the process easier and less distressing for you. With some planning and easy-to-access tactics under your belt, you'll soon be looking forward to a more peaceful future, far away from this damaged and damaging individual.

- **How to help other victims of narcissistic abuse**

Dealing with a narcissist can leave you feeling isolated and unsure of your own sanity. Read on for essential tools that will help you not only recover yourself, but also spot the signs in other victims and help them to break free, too. As more is known of this personality type, I hope to see a world where they don't get away with it nearly as much as they seem to right now. Narcissists thrive on secrecy, and by writing this book and exposing their secrets, I hope you will learn from my work and come away feeling better equipped to simply disengage from them.

Through my writing, research, and close study of this particular personality type, I have helped many people escape from narcissistic abuse. Being caught in a relationship with a narcissist is something that I liken to the "frog in the pan of water" analogy — by the time the frog realizes the water is boiling, it's too late to jump out.

With a narcissist, you find yourself struggling to escape, worn out from their mind games, tantrums, and cutting insults. You end up doubting yourself. You may feel that you are enmeshed in a seemingly endless situation and no longer have the courage to escape.

Don't let that happen to you! Educate yourself, learn the signs to look for, and how to look after yourself and others. A narcissist has the power to cause great damage and untold hurt to those around them, but it doesn't have to be that way. They are only as strong as you allow them to be.

When you truly understand this personality type, you will see that they are not nearly as powerful as they appear. You will know exactly what to say and exactly how to behave so that they simply get bored and move on to someone else. In my experience, narcissists are very difficult, if not impossible, to treat.

They don't change, and they don't seek help. Often, they are perfectly content with the status quo and resistant to any change or greater equality in their relationships with others. Why would they want change when they have everyone dancing around them?

So, as hard as it is, there's no point wishing for them to change, either, despite what they may promise you at times. They will never change. All you can do is accept that and try to move on with your own life.

With my help, you can look forward to a happier future. You can escape. You can have a life free of drama and the toxic influence of a narcissist. You can feel greater contentment and a sense of safety and purpose. More importantly, you deserve to. Narcissists are very good at playing on our better selves, on manipulating the kindest and most empathetic people to meet their own selfish needs. You don't have to fall victim to this, and you don't have to get drawn into their games.

Read on to find out how.

Chapter 1 - Unraveling Narcissism

In this chapter, we start to unravel narcissism to find out what it is, what causes it, and how to spot it in others. We also look at the kinds of people that tend to fall prey to the wiles of a narcissist.

We'll give you some clues to look out for when meeting people for the first time, and odd behaviors to look out for. Let's go!

The 7 Warning Signs of Narcissistic Personality Disorder

Narcissism is a recognized personality disorder that is thought to affect around 6% of the population, though many who suffer from it may be undiagnosed. It's characterized by a grandiose sense of self (often very much undeserved), a ruthless need to exploit others, and a strong sense of entitlement. Narcissists are also prone to narcissistic rages. Unfortunately, they keep their true selves hidden and can also be extremely charming when they need to be.

Once you know what to look for, narcissists are generally easy to spot, and you can keep them at a distance without being drawn into their world. But what are you looking for?

Read on for the 7 key signs of Narcissistic Personality Disorder if you think someone you know or are close to may have it. See if any of it rings true for you.

1.   They have a grandiose sense of self

The narcissist always has to be the best: the best looking, the most successful, the most interesting. While this can be charming or endearing in the short term, it quickly becomes wearing for those around this person, as they struggle to have their own achievements and needs recognized.

Narcissists believe that they are special and unique. They believe that they should only associate with other special people and that they deserve the best possible treatment and attention in any situation. They train others to believe this too, so that before you know it, you're dancing around this person and treating them with excessive care, often at a considerable cost to your own time, wellbeing, energy and personal growth.

They will also exaggerate and lie about their achievements, and downplay, ignore or refuse to acknowledge those of others. Whatever you may have achieved in your life, you can be certain that the narcissist has done it too — and done it better.

Classic narcissist behavior:

You: Oh, guess what? My novel is being published!

Them: That's nice. That reminds me, I'm going to write a novel. I love writing, and I was always very good at English. Everyone always told me I should write a book. Who is your agent, and can you send me their details? I would like to talk to them about my planned book.

2.   They live in a fantasy world

In their own world, they are successful, wonderful, and there to be admired. If you support and reflect these beliefs back at them, you will enjoy their approval. If, however, you dare to challenge them on the truth or details of their many achievements, be prepared for a serious backlash. You'll soon learn to tread carefully around the narcissist to avoid any repercussions or **narcissistic rage**, which knows few boundaries.

Classic narcissist behavior
If a narcissist visits your home, expect to feed them, wait on them, and clean up after them, and possibly lend them money, without any reciprocation of the favor. If you visit them, expect to be given little to eat and to simply listen to them talk about themselves. After all, you are lucky to be around them.

3. **They require lavish praise and undivided attention**

If you're in the company of a narcissist, after a while you'll start to notice something: it's all one way. You are simply there to listen to them talk about how wonderful, talented, how special they are. They want you to hear how many friends they have and how successful they are in their career.

Try and get something back from them or ask them to recognize you in any way and prepare to be frustrated: the narcissist is simply unable to pay attention to anyone else. It goes against their belief that they are the one who must be looked after, deferred to, and fussed over. They find it incredibly difficult to focus on or recognize others.

Classic narcissist behavior

You are at a party, celebrating the pregnancy of a friend. The narcissist will use the opportunity to announce their own plans to have a baby and somehow you'll end up drinking champagne and congratulating them, while they stand in the middle of the circle, smiling and enjoying the attention. Meanwhile, the pregnant friend is forgotten.

4. They have an extreme sense of entitlement

Of course, we all deserve to be treated with respect and kindness, but a narcissist takes this to another level. You may be groomed over time to accept their demands if you know them personally and accept that it's "just the way they are," but it's often jaw-dropping to see their sense of entitlement play out with other people.

Often, seeing a narcissist out in the world is a lightbulb moment for their victims. You may also see the most entitled behavior in how they treat others and feel embarrassed for them. You would be quite amazed at their ability to make the most outrageous demands, seemingly for the fun of it.

How do they treat waiters, reception staff, shopkeepers? They may be overly warm to those that treat them with deference, but watch out if someone dares to put them in their place or refuses to assist them with their often unreasonable demands.

Classic narcissist behavior

You're in a foreign city and looking for a bank. The narcissist will walk into a nearby hotel and demand that the receptionist looks up the directions of a bank, writes it down for them, and then — as an afterthought — gives them detailed instructions on various local museums. If the receptionist refuses to help them, they will feel extremely angry and become rude and petulant, and complain bitterly about how unreasonable the person was.

5. They exploit others without guilt or shame

We are all guilty at times of overstepping the mark with others, and for most people, once we realize this we apologize and make amends. We may feel shame or guilt and vow to learn from our mistake and do better next time.

But for the narcissist, there is no sense of guilt or shame. There is only rage and a sense of fierce injustice if they get called out for their behavior — after all, they are *special*. They are allowed to break the rules. Unlike normal people, the narcissist is constantly looking for a way in — and they are very good at playing on people's natural courtesy and generosity to meet their own needs.

Narcissists don't see any point in helping others for its own sake. All they care about is getting their own needs met, and they are prepared to behave as badly as they need to for this to happen. The only thing that may stop them is the worry that they are going to go too far and lose access to the person or thing they are exploiting: then, and only then, will they pull back temporarily so that they can continue to use and abuse in future.

Classic narcissist behavior

A narcissist will accept your offer to go out for the day, but will "forget" their wallet. You'll end up paying for their lunch, drinks, and entry fees. At the last moment, though, in a shop, they will suddenly "find" their wallet and buy themselves a new bag with all the money you've saved them. On the train home, they will mention that they'll pay you back, but you'll never see that money again, or even get a thank-you for treating them all day.

Or let's say you meet someone at a party who is a friend of a friend. They shower you with attention and through your friend, track down your email or phone number. Before you know it, they are passing through your town — because you had such a great chat at the party, is it OK if they stop by your house, around lunchtime? Before you know it, you're feeding them lunch and listening to them talk about themselves for two hours, lending them a book and helping them solve a problem with their phone — all on your day off.

6.   They bully, belittle, and humiliate

To control others, you need to keep them feeling small and weak, and no one is better at this than a narcissist. They are experts at hunting down your weak points or sensitivities and then using this knowledge to bully and humiliate you whenever you seem to be getting ahead of yourself. To them, it's all a game. They like making others feel small because it makes them feel powerful, and it suits them to do this to those close to them because it makes them easier to control.

Classic narcissist behavior

You're dressed up and feeling good about yourself, and the narcissist will make a snide comment about your appearance, laugh at you, or simply refuse to acknowledge the effort you've gone to. If you appear too confident, they will come out with a nasty comment about your hair or your clothes to take you down a peg.

7.   They have no empathy

This is perhaps the most chilling characteristic of a narcissist, as well as their central trait. They lack basic empathy and simply can not relate to the pain of others in any meaningful way. They may be able to fake it, but really, they feel nothing for the suffering of others. Some of the more malignant narcissists (more on this later) even seem to get some strange joy out of watching those around them suffer.

Classic narcissist behavior

You've just broken up with your boyfriend. You share the details with the narcissist and get no sympathy or comfort in return, just a bored comment about how the relationship was dragging on anyway and how you seem to always be so unlucky in love. They change the subject to talk about how well their own relationship is going.

What Causes Narcissism?

Narcissism is believed by many psychologists to have its roots in childhood. Often, it appears linked to a combination of both smothering a child with love and approval, and also neglecting them. Narcissists may have been sent to boarding school, for example, so they had holidays of luxury and privilege interspersed with long periods of institutional care where they felt alone and abandoned by their parents.

Small children tend to be quite selfish and lacking in empathy, as these are traits that diminish with maturity. The narcissist, however, never seems to learn to be kinder. They may have been overindulged as a child and allowed to get away with murder, yet also neglected by their main caregivers, never learning to feel empathy or think about the impact of their behavior on others.

Sometimes they have something happen to them that is so traumatic that they remain stuck in a selfish, immature way of dealing with others. Grown-up, but behaving like a baby. Again, this may be down to their caregivers not giving them the tools to treat others well.

As with all personality traits, it's impossible to say just how much can be put down to childhood experiences and how much is simply temperament and genes. What matters for those around the narcissist is how to deal with him or her, not what caused them to be the way they are.

It's important to remember, however, that the childhood roots of narcissism mean that it's very much a fundamental aspect of this person's nature, not something they can change, and not in any way your fault. You will find it very difficult, if not impossible, to change a narcissist. All you can do is change the way you react to them.

When is it narcissism and when is it just confidence or arrogance?

It's estimated that around 6% of the adult population suffers from narcissism. But what makes it different from the arrogance we see in popular culture? What distinguishes narcissism from the selfie culture and the self-promotion and showing off we see on social media, for example?

The difference often comes down to how authentic this confidence is — if it's genuine, it tends not to cause problems. But if it's hiding a much more uncertain person, it can be a disaster. While there is nothing wrong with demonstrating self-confidence in your life, even if it sometimes tips over into arrogance, narcissism is something different. They suffer from jealousy and are chronic "bucket dippers" — always seeking to dip into someone else's bucket of self-esteem in a flawed attempt to fill their own.

The narcissist is totally lacking in any form of self-confidence — deep down, they are actually a very small, frightened child. Their grandiose behavior is defensive and a way of protecting themselves from further harm. What looks like entitled behavior is actually an act, concealing someone with very little self-worth.

This is not true self-confidence, which is a trait that generally makes people more pleasant to be around. You can also be an arrogant person at times but still be a loving partner, for example. A narcissist, on the other hand, has a personality disorder and it's difficult, if not impossible, to have a healthy and mutually satisfying relationship with them.

4 Types of Narcissists You Need to Stay Away From

Narcissists come in different forms, and some are easier to spot than others. All, however, are worth avoiding. Here are four recognizable types and what to look for in each:

1. Overt narcissists

They make life (relatively) easy in that you can spot them a mile off. These are the kinds of people you find bragging on Twitter about their latest achievement or lying about how much their car cost, or how much they earn.

Overt narcissists are also prone to public blowups and meltdowns, which again makes them easy to look out for and avoid. They can be very charming and seductive when they want something, but once they have it, they will move on.

2. Covert or closet narcissists

These guys are harder to spot and better at concealing their true natures. They may present themselves as saint-like, doing lots of work for charity and high-profile good deeds. Scratch that pristine surface, though, or get them on their own, and you'll find a narcissist.

3. Toxic narcissists

Narcissism, like all personality traits, exists on a spectrum. A little is healthy, a bit more annoying, but a lot — dangerous.

Toxic narcissists are at the more extreme end of the spectrum, so be prepared for drama if you let one of these into your life. They may be spiteful, extremely nasty or bullying and generally make your life extremely difficult.

4. Psychopathic narcissists

I truly hope you never meet one of these characters. They are truly dangerous, showing no empathy or remorse, and actively seek to impose suffering on others. Murderers and dangerous abusers fall into this category. They enjoy the suffering of others and are vampire-like in their consumption of misery and pain.

The 4 Types of People That Narcissists Are Attracted to

One thing that you need to understand about narcissists is that they have very little sense of self. Instead of developing normal, healthy self-esteem, they ended up as adults feeling that they were both special yet very misunderstood — a strange combination, and not a happy one.

What they are drawn to, like vampires, is people with a good sense of self and a certain empathy towards others. A narcissist will want to both benefit from your kindness and also squash your self-esteem so that you give them more of your energy. They feed on the good feelings of others because they have none of their own to draw upon.

One of the terms you will hear in relation to narcissists is "supply." But what is it? Essentially, **narcissistic supply** is what they want from you — supply to them is attention, drama, focus, energy. You may have heard the phrase "she was sucking the life out of me." This is what being around a narcissist for any length of time feels like — you feel compelled to give them so much of yourself, while getting very little back, and you end up feeling exhausted.

Here are 4 of the features found in those who fall prey to the mind games of the narcissist. Keep in mind, though, that you don't have to give in to them. If you learn to spot a narcissist, you can put up good boundaries and protect yourself. In the following chapters, we'll show you how.

1.   **Someone successful and talented**

Although you'll never get the narcissist to admit it, they may target you because they perceive you to be successful or talented in some way. Unable to deal with their feelings of jealousy, they will then make a game of bringing you down, humiliating you and destroying your confidence as a way of feeling better about themselves.

Does this actually work for them? No. But remember, the narcissist is very immature. They are like a four-year-old stamping on another child's sandcastle, which they wish they had built themselves. Taking someone else down may give them some temporary relief, but soon enough, those feelings of jealousy and inadequacy will return. If you're around when they do, prepare to be attacked once again. This is the cycle of narcissistic abuse, and you will soon come to recognize that the good days are always followed by bad ones.

Narcissists will also be drawn to successful people because they feel they can ride on your coattails and draw on your connections and talents to benefit themselves — for example, turning up at your professional events and using their connection with you to meet people and try to advance their own interests.

2.   **Someone who makes the narcissist feel OK about themselves**

Again, you'll find that people who feel good about themselves tend to be willing to lend that same energy to others. So they'll give people compliments or reach out with kind gestures in the belief that this is just how you behave in life. Unfortunately for them, the narcissist will want more and more of these kindnesses, until the giver feels drained and exhausted by them. Narcissists are bottomless pits of need, and if you give them a hand, they'll take an arm.

Again, I can't emphasize enough how important it is to look not at someone's words — which can be very charming when necessary — but at how you feel around them. Do you feel on edge? Do you feel exhausted? If you are someone who tends to be kind and giving, be aware that sometimes, for your own sake, you need to hold back.

3.   Someone who makes them look good

It's not about you; it's about them. So if you have some talent, or are good looking, or impressive in some way, you may find a narcissist attaching themselves to you and feeding off your reflected glory. You may find the attention flattering, but after a while, you'll want to shake them off. That's when you realize it's not as straightforward as dealing with a normal person.

4.   Someone who indulges them and puts up with their behavior

Be careful of being too kind or understanding with a narcissist. While normal people won't take advantage of your kindness, you can be sure that this personality type will. They will essentially feed off your goodwill and attention, needing more and more of it. And if you attempt to back off or set some boundaries, be prepared for trouble.

So there you have it. With this chapter, we've looked at what makes someone a narcissist and what kinds of people they are drawn to. Read on to find out what to do if you have just realized you have a narcissist in your life!

Chapter 2 - Staying One Step Ahead

Narcissists are very skilled at manipulation, so it's all too easy to miss the early warning signs that you're in a dangerous situation with someone who seems perfectly normal and charming.

What you can arm yourself with, however, are some signs to look out for when you've just met someone and are wondering if it's "all in your head" or not. Narcissists are not quite as clever as they think they are, and you will soon learn to spot some common traits and signals.

In this chapter, we'll also look at some of the tactics used by narcissists to manipulate you, and some of the common phrases you are likely to hear from this personality type.

Finally, we'll look at narcissistic rage and its triggers. This is an important section to read as, if you haven't experienced it before, a narcissistic rage can come as a huge shock. You'll be left wondering what you've done wrong and how you can fix it.

11 Ways to Know You're in a Relationship with a Narcissist

1. They seem absolutely lovely at the start
You know what they say about something or someone that seems too good to be true. They usually are. If someone is so sweet, agreeable, and utterly delighted by everything you say and do, it should leave you feeling a little... wary. No one is that nice, right? When is this going to turn?

Trust your instincts. This cannot be stressed enough. You may be falling prey to **love bombing**, which is just what it sounds like — being absolutely smothered in love and admiration.

Don't just look at what someone says or does. Look into their eyes — does their expression match their words? Narcissists can be incredibly sweet and charming, but they can't hide their cold eyes. So, if you feel like someone's words and expression aren't quite adding up, believe yourself.

Narcissists don't want the same things from a relationship that ordinary people want. While you or I may look for company, conversation, support and shared laughter, a narcissist is focused only on what they can get from you — be that attention, glory, time, energy, money and status.

They tend to see others only in terms of what they can do for the narcissist, not as someone to share a mutually supportive relationship. So when someone seems determined to win you over, to be bombarding you with texts and declarations of affection, take a step back. Enjoy the attention, certainly, but take it with a grain of salt. Time will tell.

2. They are incredibly selfish
This is a trait shared by all narcissists, and one that plays out in big ways and small. Notice what they're like to be around — are you the one doing all the listening, or do they listen back (and by that I mean, active listening, reflecting what you say and genuinely seeming to engage with you as a person)?

Do you end up giving more — more money, more work, more emotional energy? When you come away from them, do you feel inspired and uplifted, or simply drained. A narcissist may be charming and funny, but they also have a way of taking up all the available oxygen in a room, of making everything about them. You may not notice this right away, particularly if you are someone who likes to give, but just start to notice and you may see a pattern of selfish behavior emerging.

Another point here: look at how they behave when no one is around. They may be good at the grand gestures when they have an audience, but how do they treat you when it's just the two of you?

3. They care more about the image of your relationship than the reality

Again, this is about the narcissist's obsession with appearances. Narcissists tend to be both secretive and obsessed with their public image. You may have been arguing with them that morning, but they will still post a loved-up picture of the two of you to their social media accounts and present a perfect image of your relationship to others.

With most people, life is shades of gray. But with this personality type, their need to be the best, the most popular, successful, and attractive trumps their need for any kind of authenticity. One of the things that come as a surprise to people in a relationship with a narcissist is that when they talk to others about how badly the relationship is going, they are often met with surprise.

"But she always speaks so highly of you!" is a common response. This is because narcissists want to give the impression of getting along with everyone and of sharing a wonderful intimacy with you to others. As well as wanting to preserve their image of themselves as a wonderful, popular person, this also means that others don't believe you when you say that the relationship is not as wonderful as it seems. So you end up feeling both isolated and confused — are you imagining things? (The answer is no.)

4. They are critical of everything you do

A narcissist likes to control others to feel more secure themselves, and one way of doing that is to criticize and find fault with everything that you do. The result is that you feel on edge, like you're walking on eggshells, toning yourself down to avoid further negative comments.

Be wary of those little comments about what you're wearing, your hair, your career choices, and small daily decisions — they may seem harmless on their own, but they can start to add up and chip away at your self-esteem, which makes the narcissist far more powerful than you.

If you're in a romantic partnership, look at how someone was at the start of your relationship — did they find everything you did wonderful? If that starts to change, you can doubt yourself. What are you doing wrong? How can you fix it, to get it back to how it was at the start.

Stop these thoughts! The problem isn't you.

5. You can't argue with them

With normal people, arguing may not be pleasant, but with a bit of give and take, you can either agree to disagree or move on to other topics.

Not so with a narcissist! They are simply unable to compromise or to acknowledge that they are wrong. Getting them to back down is even more challenging, and they never, ever apologize. Why would they? Doing that would be admitting they aren't perfect, and for the narcissist that is impossible to even contemplate.

6. If you disagree, you're the problem

Part of the narcissist's inability to ever admit they have crossed a line or done something wrong (which they frequently do) is that if you do disagree with them, you won't just be met with a flat refusal to acknowledge their mistake. Instead, you'll find yourself in the wrong and being attacked. Here's an example:

You: I really felt when we were out tonight that you were quite rude to me in front of my friends, and it made me feel bad.

The Narcissist: I don't know what you're talking about. That's not true. Why are you like this all the time — so angry and oversensitive?

See the difference? A normal person would listen, reflect on their behavior, and apologize. A narcissist will not only reject what you are saying; they will go further and make out that you're the one with emotional problems.

7. They don't have any close friends

A narcissist may have a lot of people around them who admire them, joke with them on social media and like their numerous selfies on Instagram. But do they have old school friends? People who have been in their life for a long time? Or is it all just superficial?

Narcissists tend to burn a lot of bridges, so if you meet someone and they appear to have no old friends at all, take note. It may be that they treat everyone so badly they are unable to maintain long relationships.

8. All their exes are crazy

As a general rule, if you hear this, run a mile. Often, the ex may well have been driven a bit crazy by the narcissist's behavior, but has since recovered and moved on. If someone seems obsessed with talking about their ex and his or her craziness, it's a big red alarm bell, and you should listen. Or you will be the next crazy one.

Also beware of the person who places all the blame on a failed relationship with the ex. Usually, a relationship fails because of shared problems or differences. It's rare for one person to be all bad and the other to be blameless. If this is how an ex is being presented, you may be in the presence of a narcissist.

9. They are suddenly nicer when you pull back

Narcissists are emotional vampires. They don't care about you as a person, but they do care, very much, about having access to your time, money, presence, and energy.

If someone treats you badly or suddenly shows their true self, it's natural to pull away. The other party may notice and apologize, perhaps, and you will both move on. With a narcissist, though, they are incapable of apology and reflection.

What they will do, though, is lure you back with kindness, extra attention, and charm. You'll know deep down that you're being played, but you'll also welcome the more reasonable behavior, feel relieved, and seek to move past it. And so the cycle will begin again.

10. They'll fight hard when you leave them
Relationships end, and it's sometimes a struggle to leave on good terms. But if a relationship has run its course, it can be done, particularly if both parties are committed to being kind and getting on with their own lives. Try and get away from a narcissist, however, and be prepared for a lot of resistance.

You may find yourself bombarded with phone calls, text messages, and even have them turning up at your door. They will also send in "flying monkeys" —people who believe the narcissist's version of events and will be convinced by the narcissist to call you up and elicit feelings of guilt and obligation to give the narcissist yet another chance. Even if they don't particularly want to be with you anymore, they will keep you dangling because they don't want to see you with anyone else.

Sometimes people decide that it's actually easier to just give in for the sake of a peaceful life — particularly if other people are being drawn into the drama — and so the cycle begins again. Once you have let them back, you can be certain that the cycle of indifference and nastiness will start again. Soon, you will probably find yourself being punished at some point for trying to break free at all.

11. You feel bad about yourself when you are around them
It's been said that you may forget what someone said to you, but you'll never forget how they made you feel. If someone makes you feel exhausted, drained, irritable, depressed, or insecure, take note. These are never good signs in a relationship.

A genuine narcissist can also make you feel frightened — in their body language and in the energy they are giving off. While their words may be conveying one thing, their physical presence and their eyes may be saying something quite different.

It's always worth listening to your gut in these situations and taking note of your bodily reactions as well as your more logical thoughts — they are equally important, and often your gut instinct is spot on.

If you notice yourself feeling anxious or on edge around someone, they may not be a narcissist, but you still need to acknowledge those feelings and set appropriate boundaries, even disengage gracefully. You don't need to have a huge showdown — sometimes, simply turning down the volume on a relationship is all you need to do to protect yourself.

Dangerous Manipulation Tactics Used by Narcissists

Narcissists have a number of tactics they use regularly to lure you into their world and keep you there. What is different from ordinary relationships is that there is always an element of control with a narcissist.

While in a typical relationship there is give and take, and a gradual building of intimacy and trust, with a narcissist it all unfolds in a way that leaves you emotionally vulnerable, weakened and at a real disadvantage. Look out for these tactics in your relationship and see if you notice anything familiar — if you do, you may well need to get yourself out of your current situation.

1.   Intermittent reinforcement

This is when someone treats you nicely, but only *sometimes*. You may put up with all kinds of shabby behavior — turning up late, showing little interest in your life, catty remarks and bullying — and then every so often, you are floored by how kind, loving, and understanding they can be.

This has a noticeable effect on your mental state. You'll feel quietly undermined by them, by their comments and behavior. You'll start to question your every move and walk on eggshells around them to avoid further criticism. You may even find yourself constantly thinking of ways to please them.

After a while, though, you might suddenly feel like you've had enough. Nothing you do seems to please them. You spend time with other people and realize how odd their behavior is in comparison. You start to wonder if perhaps you'd be better off creating some distance.

Bingo! At this point, **intermittent reinforcement** will kick in. You'll be suddenly floored by how understanding, receptive, and incredibly nice they are being. Just when you start to relax and think, *wow, they are really lovely*, the bad behavior will start again. This is a very clever tool, because people are naturally wired to go back for more when someone leaves them hanging.

Treat them mean, keep them keen, does, unfortunately, work for many of us. Another word for this tactic is **hoovering** — once they know they've gone too far, they'll start trying to hoover you back under their thumb with unexpected kindness and sweet-talking.

But this is no way to live and takes a huge emotional toll. If someone is nice to you, but only *sometimes*, take note. It's not healthy or normal behavior, and you deserve so much more. In genuine relationships, people treat each other well. If they don't, for some reason, they acknowledge it and apologize. If you find yourself being treated badly by those close to you, there's a big problem.

2. Gaslighting

This term *gaslighting* derives from the 1944 movie, *Gaslight*. In it, the abusive husband cleverly manipulates his wife into believing she is going crazy by changing her environment in all sorts of subtle ways. In her house, gaslights dim for no apparent reason, things go missing, pictures vanish from walls. She never quite knows if things are changing around her or if it's all in her head. Narcissists **gaslight** those around them regularly in all sorts of ways.

Gaslighters cause you to doubt your own sanity and keep you on unsteady ground by telling blatant lies that they then deny, making out that you are the crazy one. Some examples of gaslighting in a modern relationship might be:

Example one:

Your gaslighter tells you some unpleasant fact about yourself — for example, that you once slapped him across the face — and when you say, *no I never did that*, they say — *but you did!*

You wonder if you have simply forgotten it, or if you really did slap him across the face. You know that it's not in your nature to hit someone — yet he seems so confident that it's true. Who is right?

Example two:

Your gaslighter says he will take you out for lunch on the weekend. When you bring it up to arrange a time, he says, *no, I never agreed to that. I'm busy all weekend.*

You don't want to push it, because you know how upset he can get if he's challenged, but at the same time, you were looking forward to it. And surely, if he offered it, he would remember. Ultimately, it's easier just to let it go, but it leaves you feeling oddly mistreated.

Example three:

Gaslighting can also take place around boundaries. Let's say your friend asks if they can stay with you for a week. When after two weeks they show no signs of leaving and you push them for a definite end date, they fly into a rage about how unreasonable and unwelcoming you are being.

You wonder if you are being unreasonable. After all, they said they were only coming for a week, and now it's been two. Surely that's reasonable to ask? But they seem so angry, so maybe it is rude of you? Maybe you are being selfish, as they say. No it's not, and no you're not. You are being gaslit.

It's important to note here that people can forget what they said or be vague for other perfectly harmless reasons. But watch out if you start to notice a pattern — what is being said seems to change constantly, or you don't remember saying or doing certain things that you are being accused of, or feel like you are being manipulated somehow.

Gaslighting is incredibly difficult to call out because it's the work of people who are setting out to deceive you deliberately, not the work of fair and reasonable human beings. Really, the best thing to do if you notice gaslighting is to leave — you will never win with someone who refuses to play fair.

3. Projection

Anything a narcissist doesn't like about themselves, they will project onto you and others. So while narcissists are some of the most selfish people you will ever meet, they are also the first to accuse others of being selfish. This may be people in their circle, or it may be politicians or public figures.

For example, a female narcissist may make frequent comments about "all men being a bit stupid," but is the first to cry sexism if a man doesn't shower them with admiration and undivided attention.

They will also accuse you of being a liar if you call them out on their own lies. You will never, ever hear an admission of guilt. All you will hear is a flat denial, followed up by a declaration that you are unfairly targetting them with *your* lies.

Narcissists are unable to reflect on their behavior and admit that they are in the wrong. Far easier to dump the blame and attending shame on you, and view themselves as the wounded party.

4.   Nonsensical conversations

With most people, if you have an issue you'd like to discuss with them — perhaps to do with their treatment of you or your relationship — you would expect them to listen, reflect, and respond appropriately. Not so the narcissist! (Do you see a pattern yet?)

One of their most infuriating tactics is to shower you with **word salad** when you try and have a conversation with them about some aspect of their behavior that you are finding difficult. Prepare to be bombarded with bizarre observations, unrelated anecdotes, and strangely worded sentences that don't make much sense. You'll leave the conversation thinking — "What just happened?" while the narcissist goes on their merry way, knowing full well what they have done.

If you confront them, you'll be met with a flat denial. And, most likely, another generous serve of word salad. So really, there's no point getting into any kind of disagreement with a narcissist. It's like trying to argue with a toddler — you get nowhere.

Another thing to note here is that narcissists enjoy confrontation and argument. It fires them up to win and to leave you feeling like the bad guy. So the best thing to do is to avoid arguing with them at all — and further along, we'll learn some tactics for doing just this.

5. Vague or overt threats

Narcissists tend to be possessive and jealous, but they won't always come out and admit they are feeling this way. Instead, you'll receive a vague sense of unease if you do something they don't approve of — sulking, an angry tone, or a tantrum accompanied by threats.

Things that you would expect your friends to celebrate — a new job, some exciting personal news — will leave them feeling inadequate and abandoned. They don't like the success of others, as it draws attention away from them, so they will find all kinds of ways to burst your balloon.

If you feel you have to walk on eggshells around someone for fear of their anger, or if you stop doing things you'd ordinarily enjoy, such as going out with your friends because you're worried that you'll get in trouble, take note. This is not normal or fair behavior, and it reflects the narcissist's childish desire to have you always focused on them, and not on other things or people that make you happy.

Yes, it's a shame they react so badly, particularly if the narcissist is a family member, for example. But they won't change, so the best thing to do is to only share your good news with those you know will want to celebrate along with you. Ignore any threats and call out any sulking — you don't need to put up with it.

6. Baiting, shaming, insulting and name-calling

All of these tactics are used by narcissists, often in subtle ways that leave you wondering if you are oversensitive or just imagining things. Narcissists love to **bait**, which means saying something with the intention of hitting your weak spots or provoking anger. You take the bait, and suddenly you're being difficult and creating a drama out of nothing.

While most people, even if they know your weak spots (and we all have them) will take care to tread carefully around them, narcissists are the opposite. They will learn the things you feel sensitive about and take great pleasure in making you feel worse about them, all to make themselves feel more powerful.

Insulting and **shaming** are the same kinds of tactics — a narcissist will skilfully uncover your weak spots or things you feel self-conscious about, and then use this knowledge to insult and shame you later on. Often, this may be in the form of jokes, so that if you dare complain, you will be told you don't have a sense of humor, adding insult to injury.

5 Things Every Narcissist Likes to Say

Narcissists have a very predictable playbook, and because their tactics are so similiar, you will often here the same statements from them again and again.

1. **"That didn't happen." and "You're imagining it."**
These are both classic narcissists statements that underpin much of their gaslighting, as I described above. If you question something the narcissist has said or done in the past, perhaps in light of new information and because it contradicts what they are saying now,

they will simply deny it. Denial is one of their first defenses because unlike normal people, they have no qualms about outright lying to save their own skin.

If you can prove without a doubt that they did do something, their final defense will be that you deserved it, often for spurious or unrelated reasons (remember that they also use **word salad**).

2. "You're crazy."

Because narcissists are unable to accept their ordinary flaws and vulnerabilities, be prepared to be told you're crazy if you dare question their version of events. They may not come right out and say this, but you might find yourself being reminded of that time you got very down, or they might refer in general terms to people who are crazy but in a way that makes you suspect they are referring to you in particular.

3. "You're oversensitive."

If a narcissist goes too far in what they say or how they treat you, don't ever expect them to apologize. They are, in their own eyes, incapable of being wrong, so an apology is beneath them.

What you will hear, however, is that you are overly sensitive. Or unreasonable. Or that you have always been a bit fragile. Or again, they will mention some other time when you showed emotional vulnerability, as a way of reminding you that you aren't as strong or capable as they are (although, of course, showing vulnerability isn't weak, it's normal human behavior).

4. "It was just a joke! I'm *joking*."

As well as being oversensitive, if you take offense at one of the narcissist's cruel barbs, be prepared to find out that you have "no sense of humor" or that you "can't take a joke."

Of course, you could retaliate by pointing out that what they said wasn't actually funny, it was just nasty, bullying or plain rude, but if you do, prepare for more defensive behavior.

5.   "In my experience..."

Or variations of the above, but essentially, if you talk about something that's happening in your life, perhaps a career success or anecdote, the narcissist will always be able to top it.

If you wrote a book, they wrote a bestseller. If you had a baby, they had five. This applies not just to achievements, but also drama. If you had your purse stolen, they stood up to a bank robber and saved someone's life. What is happening here is that the narcissist is unable to bear the attention being diverted from them — they want to be centered at all times, they want to be better, they want to be the hero in every story.

You may not realize this at first, so you talk a little about yourself as well as asking the right questions and listening. But you'll soon learn to keep quiet about your own achievements because if you speak up, you'll be put in your place with a ten-minute monologue about how they did it better. It becomes easier just to keep quiet and spare yourself the boredom of listening to their boasting (again.)

5 Triggers for Narcissistic Rage

So what is narcissistic rage? Think of it as the grown-up, much scarier version of a toddler temper tantrum. While most of us get angry from time to time, we are usually able to soothe ourselves, calm down, and take steps to handle our anger without lashing out at others or doing permanent damage to our relationships.

A narcissist's rage, however, is something else entirely. These personalities just loathe being told off or challenged. Being confronted or triggered about their shortcomings is not pleasant for anyone, but it's unbearable to them, and you will be met with such seething fury that you may feel physically assaulted. Ideally, according to the narcissist, you will learn your lesson and not do it again.

Or you will be met with icy silence and quiet passive-aggressive fuming. What you won't get is a clear explanation of what's going on or a way forward.

So what incites narcissistic rage? Essentially, anything that threatens their view of themselves as a perfect, successful, and extraordinarily special human being.

Here are some surefire ways to find out just how angry a narcissist can get:

1. You confront them on their behavior

If you call a narcissist out on their behavior, prepare to suffer. Even if you make your feelings known in a way that's constructive and diplomatic, you have broken the unspoken rule that the narcissist is never wrong.

Be prepared for flat out denial, rage, projection, and blame, but be assured that you will never see any form of acknowledgment that you have a point, and perhaps they could do things differently next time. If you really do have a point and they have no reasonable defense for their behavior, their final tactic is to collapse in a heap and cry, so you look (and feel) like the bad guy.

2.   You ignore them

If you realize you are in a relationship with a narcissist and decide, for your own mental health, to back away or take some space from them, prepare to be challenged. Above all else, narcissists hate to be ignored, and if you set some reasonable boundaries around their access to you, expect them to be trampled on.

Often, this may be with someone, perhaps a family member or lackluster romantic partner, who typically shows little interest in your life, makes no effort to be around you, and makes unpleasant comments or criticism of your life choices.

But should you back off or start avoiding them, that will change. Expect to be bombarded with phone calls, emails and even unannounced visits to your home. This is because you are never allowed to call the shots with a narcissist, and you must always make them the center of attention.

And while they don't enjoy being around people in the normal sense, they also need you to give them **narcissistic supply**, which, as we have covered, is essentially your attention and energy. Should you try and take that away from them, they respond like addicts being deprived of what they need. Eventually, they will give up and move on to someone else. But before that happens, prepare yourself for a fight!

3. You laugh at them

One thing that narcissists value above all else is their public image as someone who is special, intelligent, and high status. While most people are capable of being self-deprecating or laughing at themselves from time to time, this is impossible for a narcissist. This is because it touches on their deep shame and hidden insecurity as someone who is ordinary, sometimes frightened, and not particularly special or talented. Laugh at them and prepare to be met with cold fury.

4. They don't get special treatment

Narcissists often have the people around them very well trained to treat them as if they are special and unique. But often, when they confront strangers, it doesn't go quite as they would like. They may demand special treatment from shop staff, or sit in first class when they have a third-class ticket.

When this happens, the unsuspecting stranger will soon find out just how 'special' the narcissist is and find themselves on the receiving end of verbal abuse or just more demands for attention that the narcissist actually needs or wants — they just want to make that person pay attention to them. They are the kinds of people to make rambling complaints to customer services departments, to badmouth companies with unfair reviews and to complain at length about poor customer service rather than shrugging their shoulders and taking their business elsewhere.

In personal relationships, you can also expect to see narcissistic rage if you pull back or refuse to pay special attention to the narcissist.

5. You take center stage

Let's say it's your birthday, and you want to celebrate with a meal or a birthday cake. While most people are happy to let the birthday girl or boy be the center of attention for one day, narcissists find this unbearable. Prepare for extra demands, sulking, an inexplicable tantrum or catty comments — because of course, it's all about them.

Another strange and noticeable feature of narcissists is that they are generally very bad gift-givers. Going out, choosing something that someone would love, wrapping it and presenting it to them is not something that narcissists see as worth doing. Of course, this alone doesn't mean that someone is a narcissist, but it's a common enough trait that it's worth mentioning.

What is the impact of the narcissist on you?

This is an interesting question, and one worth asking yourself. Surely, people can be difficult. Is it worth disrupting a marriage or romantic relationship or cutting regular contact with a parent because they are a narcissist? Is it not better, for the sake of peace, to simply put up with them? Breaking up families, leaving parents behind, leaving your boyfriend or girlfriend — these are all big decisions to make with life-changing consequences.

Is it better to just put up and shut up?

The answer is no. The narcissist will always have you believe that you should put up with them, that they didn't really mean it, that things will be different in the future. But they won't.

And every time you put up with it, every time you bite your tongue and attempt to get over feelings of hurt and disappointment for the sake of an easier life, you are doing two things:

You are affecting your future: your future happiness, your future goals, and aspirations, your children, and grandchildren. Every time you allow the narcissist to beat you down with nasty words and abuse, you are letting him or her rob you of a happier, more peaceful and productive life.

You are also affecting your own health and wellbeing in the moment. Of course, you just want the behavior to stop, for things to go back to normal. The easiest way to achieve that is to let the narcissist win. But play the long game. You can't see the impact of long-term, low-level stress and abuse on your mental health, but be certain it is having an impact. You have a choice to change things. And you deserve so much better.

Read on to find out how you can choose better for yourself.

Chapter 3 - When Enough Is Enough

So if you've read this far, you may have realized you have a narcissist in your life. The question for you now is, what are you going to do about it?

It may not be practical to break ties with them completely — perhaps you work with them, or they are a family member and the fall out will be too great if you cut them off completely — but what you need to do now is put your foot down. You need to change how you deal with them and prepare yourself for pushback. You need some strategies under your belt, and you need to believe in yourself enough to carry them out. Most of all, you need to heal, to practice self-care and to ensure that you set good boundaries so that you are safe from harm in the future.

You'll also learn about the Connection Contract and how this can help you get your own needs met. You may find, ultimately, that this is the first step in freeing yourself completely from a narcissist.

Read on to find out how to deal with a narcissist and protect yourself while they are still in your life.

5 Essential Tips for Dealing with a Narcissist the Right Way

Before we go much further, it's worth learning the five essential tips that you can keep in mind when dealing with narcissists. Remember, you are dealing with someone who does not have an ordinary personality. They don't follow the normal rules for human interaction, so you need to treat them differently, too. Most importantly, you need to protect yourself from harm as you set about breaking away. Here's how:

1. Keep quiet and carry on

If you are working with a narcissist, for example, you may feel like you're the only one who noticed just how superficial their charm really is. It may even be tempting to confront them, or out them to others.

Don't. Bide your time, keep your guard up around them, don't share any secrets and remain pleasant and just a little distant. In time, the narcissist's mask with start to slip and they will reveal their true selves to others. At this point, you can watch from a safe distance. But you can't force this process without putting yourself in harm's way.

If you try and make this happen faster, you run the risk of inciting their narcissistic rage and having them turn on you, and you want to avoid that at all costs for your own wellbeing.

Remember, narcissists don't play fair, and they hate being confronted with their own shortcomings. It's a game you won't win unless you stoop to their level — and who wants to do that — so simply refuse to play. You'll be on your way to making your escape, and the longer the narcissist remains unaware of your plans, the smoother your exit will be. Keep quiet, build your escape plan, and work on your own wellbeing — which we will cover in future chapters.

2. Disengage

Ultimately, what a narcissist wants is attention. Like a toddler, if they aren't getting positive attention, they will soon move onto behaving badly. If you consistently refuse to get drawn into their games, though, they will simply move on to someone else who is more willing to take the bait.

If you spot a narcissist, take things slowly and if you are proved right, be as boring as you can when talking to them. This is a great way to both protect yourself and hopefully see the back of them, too.

In some situations, you may not want to be boring. For example, in your professional life, you may want to shine and if your narcissist is in the same field, you may have to deal with some jealousy. Simply focus on doing your own work as best you can, never bite back, and be polite and professional at all times.

In personal relationships, start to step back a little, gradually. Stop taking the bait in arguments, stop expecting them to change, keep conversations light.

3.   Work our your boundaries and make them clear

This is something you may need to do if you have realized you are in a relationship with a narcissist. These personalities constantly push boundaries in all kinds of ways — imposing on your time, your energy, your privacy and your personal life. Once you recognize this, however, you'll be in a stronger position to set and maintain boundaries around what is important to you.

For example, let's say a relative constantly makes negative or belittling comments about your career. Knowing this, have a few set phrases ready when the next comment comes: such as, "Hmm. I am really happy with how my work is going. It's not always a smooth road, but I feel like I'm making progress." Deliver them lightly, without any heat at all, and know that you have just made a choice to stand up for yourself that strengthens your position and weakens that of the narcissist.

And then change the subject, or put it back onto them and ask them about how their work is going.

Or perhaps the narcissist tries to draw you into a conversation about how your life is going, and you sense some probing. Be aware that narcissists like to learn your weak spots so they can reveal them to others or bait you with them at some later date.

In this case, again, remain friendly and neutral while giving nothing away that you don't want to — remember, just because someone has asked you a personal question it doesn't mean you have to answer it. Sometimes, simply replying with "What do you mean?" or "Why do you ask?" will put an end to their fishing.

4. Don't expect fair or reasonable behavior

Narcissists are chronic game players. But they also tend to have predictable methods of attack and will try the same thing again and again if they see it gets a rise out of you. Be unpredictable in response, and work on your own strategies, which might be as simple as refusal.

If they make a nasty comment, simply refuse to accept it. State mildly, "No. That's not true."

Never expect them to be fair or kind, and have your guard up ready to bounce back. Even a long pause followed by "What do you mean?" is effective and gives you time in the moment to stand up for yourself.

Leave them feeling slightly unsure about whether you're wise to them or not. They will never play fair, so don't feel like you have to be completely fair in response — play them at their own game, but innocently.

Another good tactic here, if you have to work with a narcissist, perhaps, or see one at a family gathering, is to prepare yourself in advance. Get a good night's sleep, eat well, get some exercise and learn some simple breathing techniques that will help you remain calm and cheerful in the moment. Narcissists tend to prey on the weak, so keeping yourself strong and healthy is a good way of fending them off. We'll look more at this later on.

5.   **Accept them**

This is a hard thing to do, particularly if you are very attached to your narcissist — if, perhaps, they are your romantic partner, close friend, or parent. But if you can accept that they are a narcissist, that they cannot change and that you will never get anything different from them, your life will be easier. Part of the frustration of this personality type is that they can be so nice at times. You know they have it in them, so why can't they be like that all the time?

It doesn't matter. They can't. Often, they have no incentive to change. After all, the life of a narcissist is often superficially quite pleasant, especially with a few trained monkeys dancing around him or her. Yes, they have their demons, but they keep them well buried so mostly they are fairly content.

Accepting that your narcissist will not change is the first step in moving forward with your own life, free of their negative influence. You may not be able to shake them off entirely if they are a family member, but you will find they spend much less time under your skin than they are used to.

If you are in a romantic relationship with a narcissist, giving up on your expectations that they will change is the first step to freeing yourself, and moving on without them, or accepting them for who they are and finding other ways to get your needs met. You deserve better, after all.

5 Phrases to Instantly Disarm a Narcissist

1. **"I agree." or "You're so right."**

If you are in a work situation or family celebration, it's far easier to just go along with the narcissist. Agree with whatever they say, smile sweetly and be ever so slightly boring so that they quickly move on to someone else for more drama.

Challenging a narcissist is never really worth the energy as you will end up feeling attacked and unworthy if you do so — they cannot tolerate it, and if you try, you will soon realize just how difficult it is for them. What's more, they will seek to win the argument at any cost, and you will end up feeling attacked. Far better to smile sweetly and move on to other things — such as doing something that will make you feel good.

2. "What will people think?"

One thing the narcissist values about all else is their image. If you want them to do something for you or just behave themselves, be sure to remind them that their behavior will be visible to others.

One of way doing this is inviting other people into a situation. Let's say you're arguing with them. Say, "Look, I think I'll have a chat to so-and-so about this and see what they think" or, "Should we get Dad into the room too so we can talk about this together." They will quickly change their tune if they realize you are prepared to make others aware of their behavior and not keep it quiet.

3. "I'm sorry you feel that way."

This is a great way to defuse an argument with a narcissist. It puts their feelings firmly back onto them and is neutral enough to discourage further attacks. You aren't apologizing or taking the blame, but you are acknowledging that it is hard for them to be challenged.

4. "I can live with your faulty perception of me"

Again, this is putting the narcissist's feelings and opinions back onto them. Let's say you have set a clear boundary with a narcissist that they aren't happy with. Now, they are attacking you and saying that you're being difficult and awkward and that you should give in to them.

Instead of saying, "No I'm not!" and getting into a defensive mode, stating calmly that you can accept their faulty opinion does two things: It tells them that they are wrong, but you aren't going to bother trying to correct them. Instead, you are going to accept that *they* are wrong, and move on. It leaves them with nowhere to go because you aren't taking on their negative attitude towards you.

Essentially, you are saying that you have no interest in controlling their thoughts, even though you don't agree with them or accept them in any way — which is a healthy attitude to take towards anyone, really.

5.   "Your anger is not my responsibility."

Again, you are putting their behavior back on to them. This one may make them absolutely furious — narcissists tend to hate any form of self-help talk or what they see as new-age nonsense. Just repeat this back to them, more than once if necessary, and get away from them if you can. They will soon get bored and move on.

How to Protect Yourself from a Narcissist

Protecting yourself from a narcissist isn't easy, but there are a few tactics you can try. If you aren't yet ready to leave a relationship with a narcissist, you may want to consider forming a **connection contract** with them to get what you want from the relationship.

What's a connection contract?

Put simply, a connection contract is a written agreement setting out your baseline for how you wish to be treated. Should the narcissist break this contract, they no longer have the right to enjoy a connection with you. If you are in a relationship with a narcissist, it may read something like this:

"I don't want to listen to putdowns or be yelled at or criticized unfairly. If you are incapable of doing this, I will leave."

For a narcissistic parent who wishes to visit you, it might be more like this:

"You can stay at my house for three nights, but while you are here you are to engage positively with my children, and not yell or scream to me or anyone else who lives here. Nor do I want to give you money — you need to handle your own finances and pay for your own expenses at all times. If you can't agree to these conditions, you will need to pay for a hotel and we can meet for coffee."

Essentially, a connection contract creates a crystal-clear and neutral set of guidelines about what will be tolerated and what won't. If the narcissist breaches this, you don't need to get angry or argue, you simply point out that they have broken the contract and therefore they are no longer welcome in your presence.

Yes, it's tough and it's blunt, but it takes the pressure off you to constantly be wondering what is acceptable and what isn't. With a connection contract, everyone knows what the rules are, and if the narcissist breaks them (and chances are, they will), you can point to the contract and keep your cool.

When is it appropriate to use a connection contract?

A connection contract may come in handy when you have already had several blowups and confrontations with a narcissist, and they know that you are not happy with their behavior but they are unwilling to change or acknowledge that they have done anything wrong.

Essentially, it takes over from the arguing and sets out what you don't see as acceptable. They might read it and want to argue again, in which case you can simply say that you don't want to argue further, you just want to go with what's written down.

It's a final way of trying to get a narcissist to behave themselves, and while it may not be successful, it does at least show that you mean business.

Chapter 4 - Cutting the Cord

Why It's So Hard to Break up with a Narcissist

Let's say you've read this far and realized you are in a relationship that is toxic to your own wellbeing, and you need to get out. This may be someone you have been in a romantic relationship with, or it may be a family member or close friend you need to back away from. Whatever the situation, you need to follow some trusted strategies to protect yourself while you go through with this process.

One thing you need to bear in mind as you make plans is that getting out of a relationship with a narcissist is **not like breaking up with most people**. They don't like it, and they will make it extremely hard for you.

If you have fallen for a narcissist, you will be enmeshed in what psychologists refer to as a trauma bond. As humans, we are wired to feel close to others. So the narcissist's tactic of love bombing at the start of a relationship, or when we start to pull back, will naturally make you feel closer to them.

But eventually, a narcissist will slowly but surely turn on you. You will feel confused and insecure because you never quite know where you stand. This uncertainty makes you less confident and easier to manipulate — all tactics that the narcissist will employ without conscience to gain the upper hand in the relationship. You will feel confused because you had bonded to them in one of their nicer moments and now you are seeing a different side to them.

You may know the relationship is bad for you and that this person makes you unhappy or fearful, but somehow you have lost the courage to look after yourself and leave. You're also doubting yourself — after all, you seemed to make them so happy at first? Surely for things to change, you must have done something wrong, and if you could just work out what it was, you will get things back to how they were? And every so often they are utterly lovely, which keeps you hanging on.

Narcissists are also very good at isolating their victims, so you may feel like you have no one to turn to. This isn't true. Chances are, there are old friends or family who will embrace you if you tell them the truth about your relationship with this person. They may already be aware of the problems and are waiting for you to speak up. The fact is, relationships shouldn't be this hard.

So how did you get into this state? Well, you're human. It happens. Some of us are more vulnerable than others to the charms of the narcissist, and that is something you may need to think about in future — we will look at red flags for future relationships at the end of the book. But essentially, narcissists are very good at what they do, and at creating a trauma bond.

Trauma bonding works a little differently depending on whether it's a long-term relationship — such as with a parent — or a new, romantic partner.

With long-term relationships, it's more of a constant cycle between loving behavior and abuse that can go on for years and is established in childhood.

With romantic relationships, it tends to be that things start off well and deteriorate. Either you get out at the first sign of trouble, or you get caught into an abusive cycle that can go on for years — if you let it.

The 7 Stages of Trauma Bonding

1.   Love bombing
You are perfect and you can do no wrong, and you are won over by their charm and attention. They are flattering, kind, affectionate and seem completely in love with you. Of course, being human, you enjoy this. But of course, with the narcissist, it will never last.

2.   Trust
You believe everything they are saying, and start to trust and believe in them. While there may be some small part of you that knows it is all a bit too good to be true, they also draw you in with small acts of kindness and intimacy that make you believe and trust them. You've simply never met someone this wonderful before, and they seem to feel the same way!

3.   Criticism begins
The love bombing tails off, slowly or sometimes very abruptly, and the nitpicking and criticism start to escalate. Suddenly you are not quite so perfect. This stage may be accompanied by increasing demands on your time and energy, conflict and a feeling of despair or confusion, as you wonder what has changed, and how you can get back on firmer ground again.

4.   Gaslighting

This new state of affairs is your fault. If you just did things differently, or you weren't so crazy or irrational, it would all be just fine. You start to doubt yourself, partly because they seem so convincing. They have done nothing wrong. It's all in your head.

5. Control

You go along with what they want because you start to believe that you are in the wrong and this is the only way to get back in their good books.

6. Resignation and increased despair:

Things seem to be getting worse. If you try and fight back, you are met with more abuse. You feel lonely, sad and isolated.

7. You're addicted

You know this person is bad for you, but somehow you keep going back for more, and all you want is to win back their approval and see their kind side. With a parent, this is because we are naturally wired to love our parents, no matter how inadequate they are for the job.

With romantic relationships, it's often because we have a vision for the relationship and its future in our head, and we know it's going to be painful and lonely to give it up and go back to searching again. Far easier to stick it out and hope for things to change. You're also weakened by their constant low-level abuse and not feeling strong enough to get out.

How to Break Up With a Narcissist for Good

Breaking up with a narcissist is not an easy process, but it is worth it. Mainly because the relationship is never going to give you what you need, despite the occasional good day. You are looking for something that just isn't there. Leaving this person behind will free up space and energy in your life for better things, healthier relationships and increased happiness. You are allowed to do that — in fact, I am giving you permission right now! But how do you do it? Read on to find out.

1. Prepare yourself
Get as much information about narcissists as you can. Study this book and other resources, and know that you are doing the right thing for your own wellbeing.

2. Distance yourself gradually
Be a little less available and a little more boring. Let them think that they are getting bored of you, even, and see if you can slowly disengage rather than letting them realize what you're doing — which can incite narcissistic rage.

3. **Reconnect with others**.
This is a great way of breaking the narcissist's hold on you. Find ways of letting others back into your life, no matter how low and isolated you might be feeling. Call up an old friend, go to something that interests you, join a club. Whatever it is, break out of your isolation and surround yourself with healthy people and you'll start to feel better.

4. **Think of an excuse**
Try not to make the breakup or distancing about them. Talk about what's better for both of you, and find ways of making it seem more like their idea than yours. Don't fire them up, accuse or tell them

their faults — this is unbearable to them and will only make leaving harder.

5. Make a clean break

Don't drag it out — once you've decided to leave, go quickly. Once you've left, don't contact them again. Stay strong and don't be tempted back by love bombing, which will come. Often, with a family member, it's impossible to make a clean break without a huge amount of disruption within the wider circle of family members. In this case, it's often easier to simply move away or go low contact, which is when you keep contact to a minimum and protect yourself with firm boundaries.

Many children of narcissists will state that the best thing they did was put physical distance between them and their narcissistic parent. It broke the strong emotional hold and also allowed them to really feel safe and happy in a place with no reminders of childhood pain.

6. Expect and plan for some retaliation

You'll get people calling you, worried about you — those **flying monkeys** that the narcissist is so good at calling in. You'll get someone else trying to build a bridge. You'll receive phone calls, unexpected visits, letters with insincere apologies in your mailbox. Prepare for all of this and remain strong.

Eventually, if you remain neutral and firm for long enough, the narcissist will get bored and move on to someone else. But it will take time. While that's all going on, put in place some habits to protect you — get lots of sleep, exercise and good food to help you remain calm and focused in the face of the narcissist's outrage. We will cover this later on.

7. **Be kind to yourself**
A relationship with a narcissist can leave you feeling quite drained. You can expect some feelings of grief and a sense of loss, and even failure. These are all normal feelings and they will pass. Give yourself time and space, get some counseling if you need it, and take it easy.

Keeping a journal where you go to unload your feelings and also remind yourself of why you are doing what you are will keep you focused. When the narcissist starts love bombing, read back on your journal to remind yourself of just how nasty they are capable of being, no matter how delightful they are being right now. They won't and can't change, so getting away is the right thing to do. Remind yourself of this when you start to wobble.

Using the Gray Rock Method to Your Advantage

Above all else, narcissists love drama. They are also very competitive and envious, so if you have anything exciting going on in your life they will seek to feed off it — and try and steal away your joy in it. Narcissists love to blow out the candles on someone else's cake.

So how do you deal with this? Don't put the cake in front of them. The Gray Rock Method is a wonderful tool for dealing with narcissists. It goes against our normal instincts, but that's what you need to do when dealing with this personality type.

So how does it work?

Picture a gray rock. No color, no life, nothing to see here. And then, quite simply, behave like one. It's as simple as that. This trick is essentially making yourself appear so dull, so boring, that the narcissist has nothing to feed on and will soon (hopefully) move on to someone else.

What narcissists want is your energy. If you are feeling good, they want to take that from you. If you have some exciting news, they want to top it. If you have something painful going on in your life, they want to get up close and see your pain. They are the true definition of emotional vampires.

Give them nothing but a boring gray rock.

When they come back to you, looking for shiny treasures to steal, continue to give them nothing. Respond to their requests for information with boring small talk. Never tell them what's going well in your life, because they'll find a way to ruin it for you. If they probe, just tell them it's all been pretty quiet. No news.

Gray Rock is a good way of getting yourself written out of the ongoing melodrama that is the narcissist's life. They'll need to go looking elsewhere for their fix, and you'll be free to enjoy a more peaceful existence.

This is hard to do. There's always going to be a part of you that wants to win them over — particularly if they are a parent. After all, aren't they supposed to be happy for their children? Isn't that normal?

Yes, it is normal. The thing you have to remember, though, is that you don't have to be a good person to become a parent. In fact, you can be a thoroughly unpleasant person and have lots of children. It's a sad fact of life that the most undeserving people can be blessed with children, but they are emotionally unequipped to love and care for them.

Thankfully, this isn't the case for most of us. But if you drew the short straw, you are better off accepting it and looking for love and approval elsewhere than trying to get it from someone who doesn't have it in them, even if they are your mother or father.

With a romantic partner, you may find yourself wanting to impress them, to win them over and get things back to how they were at the start. Sadly, you can't. Their initial charm was an act, and what you are seeing now is their true self. Stop trying to win them over, and put your energy and time into building a happier future, far away from this damaged soul.

A note for your future self.
Chances are, you won't get into another relationship with a narcissist in a hurry. You have learned your lesson, and you'll know to pull away the minute you see signs of love bombing or sudden nastiness (more on this later.)

But here's a powerful quote from writer Maya Angelou to keep you safe:

"When someone shows you who they are, believe them the first time."

Chapter 5 - Healing From Narcissistic Abuse

If you are reading this book, chances are you are feeling bruised and attacked as a result of the interactions you've had with the narcissist in your life.

Psychologists now recognize that emotional abuse — the kind that you cannot see and leaves its bruises on the soul, not the body — is just as damage and traumatizing as physical abuse. Those who have experienced it often say they would rather be hit physically because wounds to the psyche are far more painful and debilitating.

It's also now recognized that psychological abuse can lead to the same kinds of trauma that result from single traumatic events, such as a burglary or mugging. Because the narcissist's abuse takes place over a long period of time, it can be hard to see the wounds and damage you have sustained. Instead, victims have a feeling of having been attacked or wounded that will take an equally long time to heal from.

Survivors of single incidents like car accidents know this instinctively, and while the damage can be deep, you can recover. The difference with narcissistic abuse, however, is that you may on some level feel it was your fault. The narcissist is very good at making you doubt yourself, at planting little seeds of uncertainty, all the while painting themselves as blameless. It's no wonder you feel like you're under siege or suffering from deep trauma when you encounter a narcissist.

In this, the most important chapter of the book, we will turn our attention from the narcissist and back to where it should be — on you. We will look at the stages of recovery from narcissistic abuse, and how each one will play out.

We will also reveal the transformative truths that every victim must face up to if they are to recover from their experience. Plus, we will provide you will some essential exercises to strengthen and heal your mind and heart.

Finally, we will offer you life-altering affirmations to heal past hurts and to repeat to yourself like a mantra as you begin the exciting process of moving on from this toxic relationship and starting the next, happier chapter of your life.

The 5 Stages of Recovery from Narcissistic Abuse

Recovering from narcissistic abuse is similar to recovering from the death of a loved one. Particularly if you have loved and believed in this person for a long time and been taken in with their stories, it is hard to accept that they aren't who they said they are in. In fact, they aren't even close to how they portray themselves.

Recovery can be broken down into five stages. To some extent, your healing process will depend on your personality and the narcissist in your life. It's also important to note that there may not be a moment when you say you are completely over what has happened. Abuse leaves scars, and even if they heal over and no new ones are formed, they are still there. But they will make you stronger and more compassionate, so don't feel like you are changed for the worse, or irreversibly damaged. You have simply changed and grown up a little more, as we all do (apart from narcissists!)

Here is a rough guide that will help you understand the recovery process better.

Stage 1: Emergency mode

Let's say you've had what you expect to be your final showdown with the narcissist. You've told them it's over, you've left the building or put down the phone, and you are determined that you won't let them back again.

You might be getting messages from them or have them turning up at your door. Or you might be hearing from them through other concerned bystanders, sent in by the narcissist to play on your guilt, fear, obligation, and sympathy.

What you need right now is emotional safety. Talk to someone who understands the narcissist and won't place any blame on you. Tell yourself you are doing the right thing. And most importantly, do nothing to punish yourself. No bingeing on food, no ruminating or self-blame, no alcohol or drugs.

Practice **radical self-care**: treat yourself as you would a loved one who has suffered an injury. Here are some suggestions:

- Provide yourself with rest, good food, warm baths and even a bunch of flowers. Shop for and cook your favorite comfort food.
- Get some fresh air and gentle exercise.
- Listen to uplifting guided meditations on YouTube.

- Keep busy, put your house in order with some decluttering.
- Go for a swim or whatever exercise makes you feel good.
- Read a book or watch a funny movie.
- Make some plans for the future — a journey, a project, a new area of study.
- Get back in touch with nature: a walk in the forest or by the beach, or just a trip to your local park. Whatever it takes!

You can see from this list that it's about getting back to basics: doing the kinds of things that make a small child feel good. Keep it uncomplicated and know that you are doing the right thing by looking after yourself.

Switch your phone off if you need to and stay away from social media, where you may find your abuser trying to track you down. At this stage, you may be traumatized from the abusive contact and it's crucial to focus on calming yourself.

Stage 2: Moving forward and getting angry

Here, you'll start to feel your energy returning and you may have moments of rage and anger as you realize just how much time and energy the narcissist stole from you.

You might also feel angry at yourself — for letting the narcissist get away with their behavior for so long, for not speaking out or standing up for yourself. This is all totally normal and just means that you are moving forward and growing, not that you have failed or done anything wrong.

1. The narcissist will never change in the way you need them to

Obviously, everyone is capable of change and personal growth. We all develop in all kinds of ways, some of us more than others. But the narcissist is very resistant to change, and you should never waste your time and energy hoping that things will be different.

For a start, it leaves you stuck in a position of waiting. And people can stay in that place for years. You may have moments when you see the possibility of things being different — for example, the narcissist has behaved badly, you have shut them out, and they are now luring you back in with promises that this time things will be different.

They won't. All that will happen, if you let that person get close again, is that the cycle will begin one more time. And then again and again. Even if they were to change, perhaps after many years of therapy, they will still be lacking in basic empathy. And do you really want to spend years of your one precious life waiting for someone to be better? All that time, all that energy, could be far more productively spent on other endeavors and more deserving people.

2. They aren't a different person with others and it wasn't you that was the problem.

Don't believe you are the only one to struggle with this person, although they may make you feel that way. Yes, it may seem like all is well in their other relationships, and you were the one that caused problems. But they aren't different towards other people. They are the same person with everyone.

The only difference is that you are seeing the outside of those other relationships, not the inside. Narcissists are incapable of treating anyone with kindness and decency. But they are also both secretive and obsessed with image, so chances are, their other relationships are also lacking and toxic, but they just hide it well.

3. They abused you deliberately and it wasn't "all in your head"

Because narcissists are so good at what they do, and at keeping their tricks just below the radar, you may start to wonder if you are imagining things. You might wonder if they are genuinely nasty and abusive, or if they somehow don't quite realize that what they are saying and doing is hurtful.

Yes. They know exactly what they are doing. There is no excuse for their behavior, although you will probably hear a few excuses: they are getting older (elderly narcissists are very good at hamming up their age when it suits them), or perhaps they had an unhappy childhood and you should actually feel sorry for them.

No. Sorry. Not good enough. Plenty of people have miserable childhoods and don't go around making others feel bad. There is no excuse for abusive behavior. This pity party is something that narcissists are very good at throwing when it suits them, particularly to target empathic individuals who will feel sorry for them and forgive them their behavior — only for it all to start up again one more time.

What compassionate people find hard to understand about narcissists is just how much pleasure they get from manipulating, exploiting and playing with others. Most of us don't enjoy those things and find it hard to imagine feeling happiness at the suffering of others. But narcissists do. They feed off the drama, the misery, and it gives them a sense of power, control and meaning in their otherwise empty lives. Sadly, there is no getting away from this, no higher self you can appeal to in the soul of a narcissist.

Nor is their abusive behavior accidental. A good question to ask yourself, if you are wondering about something a narcissist said or did, is — who was with you when they said that? Were you alone? Or did they say it in front of others? Anyone who can change how they behave depending on who is listening knows exactly what they are doing.

And even if they are unwell, it's not your problem. You have the right to protect yourself and live a life free of narcissistic abuse.

4. Recovering will take time and isn't a process you can rush

Unlike a single traumatic event, such as a car crash, narcissistic abuse takes place over a long period of time. While physical wounds can heal, damage to your mental health takes longer.

What this means is that you don't have to forgive your abuser or sweep your feelings under the rug.

If you feel sad or angry about how you were treated, that isn't a sign of weakness. It's a reasonable response to what has happened to you.

Nor do you need to forgive or feel compassion for your abuser. After all, they feel no compassion for you.

The narcissist wants you to doubt yourself, to minimize what happened and to believe that you are exaggerating or making it out to be worse than it was. This isn't true. Narcissists are truly dangerous and disruptive people, and you can take as long as you need to in healing from your experience.

5. All emotions are valid

There is no right way to feel. You may have felt, with your abuser, that certain feelings or reactions were unacceptable. Narcissistic parents are very good at training their children to subdue emotional responses and never complain, for example.

But all of your emotions are valid, and you have the right to feel them and express them appropriately, whatever they are. You have the right to feel **angry** for what has been said and done, as long as you aren't expressing your anger in a way that is destructive to others.

The trick is to use your anger productively: Use it to drive you forward, to energize you and to put your feelings into things that will further your own life. It can be a creative force for the good if you channel it and use it wisely!

You also have the right to feel **grief**. This isn't a weakness, it's an acknowledgment that you have lost someone you cared about, or at least the idea of who they were to you. Feel your grief, honour it, and move forward.

It can be helpful to take some distance from your emotions, to see them as separate to you: perhaps visualize your emotions as clouds that move through the sky. In the same way, they move through your body and simply pass. You don't need to fall apart: simply feel them, acknowledge what you are feeling, and let it sit with you for as long as you need to.

If you want to shift an unhelpful emotion, here are two things you can try.

• Bodywork: We hold emotions both good and bad in our body — just think of how differently we look, move and sound when we are feeling happy and when we are sad. So it makes sense, then, that bodywork is a way of shifting emotion. This might be through massage with a skilled therapist, yoga, meditation or a long walk. Swimming and being close to the water is also very healing for our emotions.

• Talking to a therapist skilled in post-traumatic stress disorder is also helpful as you work through emotions, and they will have specific techniques you can use to move forward.

Essential Exercises to Strengthen the Healing Heart & Mind

As you begin your healing journey, you may find journaling your thoughts and feelings useful. This can be a brain dump style of journaling, where you simply get all of your thoughts and memories out of your head and onto your page, or it can be a guided series of questions to help you ask yourself how you got into your relationship with the narcissist and what you have learned.

Read on for some simple writing exercises that will clarify your inner thoughts and feelings and make moving forward a little easier by asking you some questions about your experience.

Find a time when you won't be interrupted and you are feeling strong, curious and ready to move forward in a significant way to get the most out of this exercise. Take as long as you need to, and feel free to return to these questions and your answers when you feel uncertain or upset. You will find your answers and your own inner wisdom very powerful. Ready? Let's go!

1. What are your false beliefs about the relationship?

Here, you can note down anything you believed about the person and your relationship with them that you now feel is false. Here are some ideas about things that you may have believed:
- Did you feel the problems were all your fault? None of us are perfect, but everything can't have been your fault. Start to unpick this and see if you gain a clearer picture of your relationship.
- Did you feel there were things you could have done to change the relationship?
- Did you feel he or she treated others better, or in fact does he or she treat everyone with a degree of contempt?
- Do you feel you will never find someone else? Is this true? Do you have other people in your life who care for you?

2. Is there anyone in your childhood who encouraged you to take on the blame?

- Sometimes, with a narcissist, we find ourselves taking on the blame for everything that has gone wrong, while the other person gets away looking like the innocent party.
- Is this a pattern from your childhood? Does it feel familiar to you? Is it true, or, like most children, were you just doing the best you could and making a few mistakes along the way?

3. What do you get out of protecting your abuser and taking the blame?

Perhaps you have some idealistic picture of how your relationship with this significant person should be, and you want to hold on to it. Perhaps you fear that if you stand up for youself you'll end up alone.

What is holding you back from facing up to the truth and leaving this person behind?

4. What are some alternative viewpoints you could come up with?

Finally, look at all the beliefs you have written down in part one, and come up with some alternatives that are realistic and feel true to you. For example, if you felt like it was all your fault, write down the ways in which you tried to make things better. Then list down the things that definitely weren't your fault and were simply the narcissist behaving badly.

Use this writing to return to when you are wavering or overcome with self-blame for what has unfolded. Taking the time to reflect on what has happened and challenging the status quo and the story your narcissist has told you is a way of replacing unhealthy beliefs with ones that are kinder and will help you move forward.

Life-Altering Affirmations to Heal Past Hurts

Add to your journal some affirmations that resonate with you, and use these to strengthen you when you are feeling overwhelmed. Again, this is something for your own private use and you can use it however you like, in ways that feel helpful and appropriate to you.

1.   "I am healing."

This is perhaps the most powerful affirmation and one that you can use to counter any negative thought spirals when they come up. Healing is a long, slow process, but it can and does happen.

Healing may not be a straightforward or linear process, and there will be setbacks along the way. But you will heal.

2.   "The past is behind me, and I am focusing on the present and the future."

It's easy, particularly when you are having a bad day, to get stuck in the past: regrets, rumination, thoughts about what you could have done differently or reliving horrible moments with the narcissist. Forgive yourself when this happens, and commit to the present and the future.

When you do get stuck in the past, the above affirmation can keep you steady. There is nothing any of us can do to change the past. All we can do is acknowledge what happened and use what it taught us to drive us into a happier future. It's also a good reminder to value the present moment.

3. "There is absolutely nothing wrong with this moment."

Again, the past can rear up to haunt us at vulnerable moments. When that happens, focus on the present. Stand outside, listen to the birds, feel the sun on your face and remind yourself that you are safe and free from harm.

4. "I am a loveable person who deserves to be treated with respect and kindness."

This is the belief that narcissists are so very good at trying to dismantle. They are incapable of offering others love, respect, and kindness, or of feeling these things within themselves, so they do their best to make you feel like you don't deserve them, either.

Once you get away from a narcissist, you will need to work hardest at this affirmation. It means exactly what it says, and it is true!

5. "I deserve self-care."

This one is a life-long affirmation. We talked a little about self-care earlier in this chapter, and it is something that will really help you on your healing journey. It's also a way of putting yourself first — not all the time, of course, you're not a narcissist — but enough that you feel looked after and loved.

This isn't a selfish act; it's actually a way of ensuring you can take good care of others too. You can't fill up the tanks of others, such as your children and friends, when your own tank is running on empty. So look after yourself.

6. "I know what I know, and I trust myself."

Narcissists are experts at gaslighting and manipulating, making you doubt your own reality so they feel more powerful.

This affirmation seeks to counter that by putting you in charge of your own head and encouraging you to trust and believe your own intuition, thoughts, and feelings.

7. "I have the right to boundaries."

Protecting your boundaries is another act of self-care that you will need to work on as you recover from narcissistic abuse. It's particularly important as you can expect that the narcissist may lay low for a while, but will always return at some point to have another go at you.

Remain strong and unyielding, and quietly protect your boundaries at all times.

8. "They don't miss me; they miss the power."

If you feel sad for the narcissist because they seem lonely or try and get back in touch with you, remind yourself of who they really are with this affirmation. They never really loved you. It's not because of anything you did wrong, but because they simply aren't capable of love. What they do miss is having the power to mistreat you.

9. "My success is my response."

When anger strikes — and it will — don't lash out at them. This is exactly what they want you to do, as if you are showing emotion it means they still have power over you. Instead, repeat the above affirmation and use its energy to do something positive in your new life: work goals, a creative project, an exercise goal, or some self-care.

Work on things in your own life and let your happiness and future success be your revenge. Karma has a way of unfolding in its own sweet time — so you don't need to give it a push. You're too busy with other things.

10. "I have good friends and family around me."

As well as repeating this to yourself, seek out those who make you feel good and who you love and trust. Being around a narcissist is like being in a cold, dark room. Look for those people who make you feel like you're standing in a warm pool of sunlight, who treat you with kindness and warmth. Good friends and loving family members are the best antidotes to a narcissist you will ever meet. These can also include work colleagues, neighbors and the new people who appear unexpectedly when you make room for them — all those people in your life who treat you with respect and kindness. Treasure them, enjoy them and keep faith that they are out there.

Chapter 6 - Breaking the Cycle

In this chapter, we want to talk about how you can avoid narcissists in the future. We will look at why you might attract the attention of narcissists and how you can spot a narcissist

Finally, we'll get creative and provide you with some methods for developing self-love and self-care, along with various practices to cultivate inner peace and happiness. These techniques will not only make you feel good, they will also provide you with protection against any narcissists in your life. Let's get started.

6 Reasons Why You Keep Attracting Narcissists

First of all, I need to clarify the above statement. It's estimated that around 6% of the population suffers from Narcissistic Personality Disorder. So if you are out and about a lot, working, going out and meeting people in your daily life, chances are you will come across a narcissist or two.

The trouble isn't encountering them or even attracting them. Because they burn through relationships more than most people, they also tend to hone in on anyone new, seeking fresh attention. The problem is letting them hang around. Narcissists are very good at spotting those who are going to put up with them, and who are therefore ripe to be exploited. So it's not about attracting narcissists — we all do at times — it's about letting them in your door.

Here are some questions to ask yourself about why you may have accepted a narcissist into your life that will help you both understand yourself better and be more aware in future about what to look for at the start of a relationship.

1. Do you tend to put up with other people's selfishness?

Some of us are more tolerant than others, and if you suffer from low self-esteem or were raised in an environment where you were expected to accommodate selfish behavior, such as that of a parent, you may be conditioned to put up with selfishness. Narcissists will very quickly work out who will put up with their games and who won't and will hone in on those who tend to be more accepting and easy-going.

You don't need to be too wary or suspicious — after all, most people aren't narcissists. But don't feel you have to let everyone in straight away. Taking the time to get to know people slowly is a better strategy and if you do notice someone seems a little selfish — dominating in conversation, letting you pay for everything — take note and slow down in what you give them.

2. Do you have boundaries around what you will and won't tolerate from others?

This can apply to friends, family and romantic partners equally. If you are someone who tends to feel taken advantage of, you may also be a target for narcissists. Look first at your own treatment of others — are you respectful of others, do you ensure you treat everyone as you would like to be treated yourself? Once you know you respect other's boundaries, why not insist that your boundaries are also protected?

This means thinking about how you would like others to treat you, and speaking up when you aren't happy about something. It's something you can learn to do, so if you feel like this may be one of the things that the narcissist saw in you, look into ways of strengthening your boundaries — we will cover some here, but a few sessions with a therapist is a great starting point.

3. Do you tend to stay for longer than you should in a bad relationship?

Backing out of a relationship that started off well but has since gone downhill is not always easy to do. At what point do you end it? How do you go about it? Should you stay, just to see if it improves?

If you are someone who finds it hard to know when to finish something, when to let go and move on, you may sadly be someone that narcissists are drawn to. If you feel that a relationship hasn't turned out as you would like, and you are unsure about whether you should leave or stay, there are a few things you can do.

First of all, remember that relationships are always changing. They get better or worse, but they never stay the same. The trick is to look at the pattern — if the relationship started off well but has steadily worsened, and you are feeling bad about yourself, then it's time to step away. It's simply not worth your precious time and energy to stay in a relationship that isn't making you happy. Never.

4. Are you someone who puts up with being devalued?

A narcissist will always start out lovely and charming, but let them in, and you'll start to see their true self. This may start with a subtle put-down or slightly off comment. Or you may realize that they never have their wallet during dates. Overall, they seem to always take more than they give in terms of time, energy, and effort.

If you are someone who has a tendency to put up and shut up, you are the ideal target for a narcissist. This doesn't mean that you have to get into a shouting match with them when they behave badly, it just means that you need to watch out for this tendency to be too much of a people-pleaser. Ensure that the people you bestow your time and kindness upon truly deserve it, and give it back, too.

5. Do you tend to excuse other people's bad behavior?

It's good to give people the benefit of the doubt. Everyone has bad days and no one is perfect. But if someone's behavior is consistently difficult and you find you are always trying to find an excuse for it, this is a big warning sign.

6. If someone is abusive, do you leave immediately?

This, more than anything, is a huge red flag. We all have different levels of what we will tolerate, depending on how we were raised and our own temperament and personality. If someone grew up with a parent who was violent, for example, they might have been groomed to see this behavior as acceptable or simply what happens in relationships.

If you feel you are someone who puts up with more than you should, get curious about this. Talk to a therapist or do some reading about what constitutes emotional abuse as well as physical abuse. Learn more about listening to your gut instinct and the warning signs of abuse. All of these things can be learned and will protect you from harm in the future.

7 Ways to Spot a Narcissist on the First Date

As we now know, narcissists are good at charming others, at seeming incredibly caring and understanding — until you get to know them. Then, it's a different story. But how do you filter them out before you get hurt? It's not easy, feeling a connection with someone makes it even harder. Fortunately, there are some warning signs.

1.   They have planned out the date out in detail

People who can't plan anything can be frustrating and at first sight, someone who seems to be in control of every detail of a first date may be a welcome change.

But pay attention to those early interactions — do they let you choose the venue, or do they insist on deciding? When you get there, do they say "Would you like me to order?" or do you make that decision together?

Someone who seems to want to be in control of every detail may be simply organized, or they might have a controlling and narcissistic personality. It's too early to tell either way — but just be curious, and take note.

2.   Love bombing

We've already looked at this in detail, but it's worth mentioning again as it's such a typical narcissistic trait, and one that can easily win you over if you aren't clued into it. If your date agrees with absolutely everything you say, something is up. No one is that nice or that agreeable. While it's flattering to have someone so seemingly in tune with you, if you start to feel like you're being played, you probably are.

Also look out for dates who start making too many plans, too quickly. On a first date, you should feel like you have a little time to breathe and reflect afterward, not find yourself lining up another meeting straight away.

Narcissists are very good at charming people and then before you know it they are in your life, settling in and taking over your time, your energy and your money. Be cautious. If something seems too good to be true, it usually is.

3.   Lots of subtle bragging

It's an interesting fact that those who genuinely have the most to brag out — wealth, success, talent, beauty — tend not to brag at all. Instead, they seek to make others feel good because they have no need to seek approval from others themselves.

The out-and-out braggers are easy to spot and almost comical in their efforts to boast and impress with their money, power and success. But watch out, too, for the humblebraggers and the stealthy boasts that gradually add up to a picture of someone who feels that they're superior to everyone else. These are the really skilled narcissists, and if you noticed a few too many brags, you may be in the company of one.

4.   **They are rude to staff**

How someone treats wait staff and others who are there to serve is always telling. Do they demand, complain and act superior, or do they make jokes on their behalf or try to humiliate them? Do they insist on sitting in a particular spot, or have some kind of problem with the restaurant's environment? If you see someone doing these things, it's a big warning sign that they may soon treat you the same way.

Being rude or getting angry over everyday annoyances like slow service in a restaurant is also a sign that they may have problems with anger management. Sure, everyone has bad days and gets annoyed, but if someone seems to have no sense of perspective and can't keep their cool in public, you may have a problem.

And also look out for anything weird around money — as we have discovered, narcissists tend to be bad gift-givers and are often stingy with money. Red flags here include suddenly disappearing to the restroom when it's time to pay the bill, refusing to leave a tip, or forgetting their wallet.

5.   **What they say they want and their history don't add up**

If someone acts like they are desperate to settle down, marry and have children, be cautious. No one should be talking long-term on a first date (or second, third, or fourth...) Dig a little deeper and ask about someone's recent romantic history. Do they have a series of short-term relationships and dramatic breakups behind them? Do they have ex-partners that they still talk about a lot? All of these points may mean that you are in the company of a narcissist who tends to churn and burn through romantic partners.

6. They get you to reveal your insecurities but guard their own

Narcissists are very good at probing and digging around to find your weaknesses and the things you feel a little sensitive about. In time, they will use these to make themselves feel more superior and to needle you when they want to put you in your place.

Yet, you will never see them admitting their own insecurities in any meaningful way. While you spill your secrets, they will simply listen, smile and perhaps say something cutting to twist the knife a little.

If you come away from a date feeling like you've been way too candid and vulnerable, it may be a sign that you've just met a narcissist. Meeting new people should make you feel good, uplifted, encouraged — it shouldn't make you feel small or exposed.

7. It's all about them

The best conversations are a two-way street — some listening, some talking, some shared laughs, and observations. But not so with the narcissist, who isn't there to learn, listen and enjoy, but to be admired and fawned over. If someone talks non-stop, and you find yourself needing to disappear to the restroom just to get a break from their incessant chatter, be warned — this is your future.

If every anecdote you tell seems to segue into a similar story about something they did, but better, it's yet another warning bell.

Narcissists find it very hard to listen. Usually, they seem distracted, they fiddle with their phone or don't quite meet your eye. They prefer to be discussing their own skills and talents than learning more about the people around them. If it's all about them, prepare yourself for the possibility that you may be in the company of a narcissist.

Another thing you might notice is that they talk very flatteringly of other people they know — friends, work colleagues, family members. You feel yourself getting ever-smaller in comparison to these wonderful people, and wonder why you are spending a date hearing about how special someone else was — shouldn't there be some focus on you? (Answer: yes.)

What to do if you realize all this on the first date?

Don't panic. Enjoy the evening for what it is (a learning experience!) and be sure to debrief with a trusted friend afterward. Spotting a narcissist early and setting up your boundaries accordingly is a useful life skill and one that is worth knowing!

4 Ways to Stop Attracting Narcissists Once and for All

If you feel like you keep attracting this type of person into your life, you are probably desperate to halt the pattern. After all, why would anyone want to invite such difficult people into their lives?

The truth is, the narcissist is there to teach you something. And until you learn it, they will keep coming back. See them as a teaching tool and they are suddenly so much easier to deal with. But what are they there to teach?

Essentially, it's people-pleasers that seem to attract narcissists. Docile, easy-going types are their favored prey. If this is you, there are ways you can change this dynamic.

1.   Don't make so many excuses for people

If someone behaves badly, they are in the wrong. Full stop. It doesn't matter how hard their childhood was, how stressful their job is — there is no excuse for abusive behavior. Don't excuse it. Don't empathize. You aren't their doctor and you aren't their punching bag. It's not your problem and you can't fix anyone but yourself.

Yes, it's hard to walk away from people. It's hard to accept that you can't fix someone, even if you care for them. It's hard when you know how forgiving you are, how kind and how good the relationship would be, if only they weren't so nasty. But you need to put yourself and your own physical and emotional safety first.

If someone is abusive towards you, walk away. It truly is the key to a happy and safe life, and you deserve it.

2.   Spot the red flags and trust your instincts

We have covered red flags in detail, and you are now well-armed with a checklist of signs to look out for.

Take note of them, trust your instincts, and if you feel like you aren't safe, back away. Resist the urge to stay in a situation that makes you uneasy because you don't want to be rude or cause trouble.

You don't have to tell the person why you are no longer available — in fact, with a narcissist, it's better that you don't, as they love confrontation and showdowns. Simply back away, disengage and make it clear that your time and energy are being taken up elsewhere.

3.   Don't let yourself get overpowered

Something narcissists are very good at is wearing down their victims. This may be with long, exhausting conversations where you literally cannot escape. It may be by waking you up early or keeping you up late at night so you feel tired and less able to make clear decisions. It may be by keeping you under close scrutiny — watching what you do, asking lots of questions and making lots of comments so you feel self-conscious and targetted.

Be aware of this tendency, and if you feel yourself getting swamped, find a way to free yourself. Get off the phone, go to bed early, go home. Take some time and space to re-energize — a swim, a workout, some meditation or a long walk — and then deal with them. If a narcissist knows that you have clear boundaries around your time and energy, they will move on to someone else.

If it's a good, healthy relationship, they won't mind you taking things slowly.

4.   Seek help from a skilled therapist

If you find yourself involved in these relationships again and again, it may be that you need to unpick the deeper reasons with the help of a skilled therapist. This will take time and money, but it may be the best investment you ever make in yourself and your future.

9 Powerful Tips for Developing Unbreakable Self-Love

A tried-and-tested way to protect yourself from narcissists is to develop self-love. This isn't about being egotistical or narcissistic yourself; it's about looking after yourself in the same way you would a good friend or a small child. Here, I've gathered together some simple techniques and ideas to really work on your self-love.

This is something that a narcissist cannot take away from you, and that will keep you safe in the future.

1.   Start each day by setting mindful intentions

Intention setting is essentially telling yourself you are worthy of care and love. Start each day with a few moments of mindful breathing and set your intention for the day, which may be something as simple as "Today I am going to take care of myself and show myself love in everything I do because I deserve it."

It may sound strange, but say this — or create a personal message or mantra that works for you — and you will see the benefits. Essentially, a loving mantra or intention sends a signal to your subconscious that you are worthy of love and care that slowly but surely challenges all those negative messages that were given to you by the narcissist.

2.   Treat yourself as a friend or small child

If you are feeling down about yourself and can't seem to shake off feelings of low self-esteem, think of yourself as someone else — perhaps a good friend or a small child. What would you do to make him or her feel better? What would you advise? If you were a wise and compassionate friend, what would you tell yourself to feel better? If you were looking after a small child, would you feed her a good meal, run her a warm bath and give her a comforting story in bed?

Writing a letter to yourself is another powerful way to tap into your inner wisdom and kindness. Write down everything you would say to yourself and when you read it back later, you'll be amazed at how powerful your words can be. Keep your letters and read them back to yourself when you need clarity or a bit of support.

3. Acknowledge your feelings

Somethings, simply naming your feelings — *I feel sad*, or *I feel regret* — can be a way of moving through them. We are very good at escaping our feelings in all sorts of ways: numbing out on social media, alcohol, shopping, overeating.

But sometimes taking the time to really feel them — sitting with them, going for a long walk or swim, or writing them down — is the best way to integrate and learn. Instead of always trying to escape, befriend your feelings and you will soon find that they are simply feelings, not a concrete, fixed reality, and they will pass.

4. Treat yourself in healthy ways

Life is here to be enjoyed and savored. If you have found yourself in a relationship with a narcissist, you may have forgotten this. You may be feeling worn out, discouraged and small.

Take back control and treat yourself with acts of kindness and positivity, as you would someone who is recovering from an illness or accident. What are your favorite ways to relax — a funny movie, a holiday, your favorite home-cooked meal in front of the TV, a hot bath or a long swim or walk in the forest?

Make a priority of yourself for a change — do all those things that make you feel good, and leave time to do them regularly.

5. Meditate

The benefits of meditation are now well known, and regular meditation is a surefire way to boost feelings of calm, happiness and control. Thanks to the internet, it's easy to meditate — just search for guided meditations online, find a quiet space to sit or lie down, and give yourself ten minutes or longer to meditate — you'll soon notice the benefits of increased clarity and joy.

6. Feel gratitude

It's easy to get ground down by everything that goes wrong, particularly if you have a narcissist in your life reminding you of your every flaw and failure. But research consistently shows that it's feelings of gratitude, not money, wealth or success, that lead to good self-worth.

Take a moment when you remember to think of everything in your life that you feel grateful for — your friends, your health, everything that went well that day, from a small conversation to a quiet moment to reading a good book. Feeling gratitude for the small pleasures of life is the true key to happiness.

7. Look after your body

While focusing on meditation and healthy self-talk will take care of your mind, don't forget about your body. Eating well, drinking lots of water, getting enough sleep and getting some regular exercise — even if it's just a gentle walk or a ten-minute workout video or dancing around the house — are all essential for happiness.

It's so easy nowadays to live in our heads — online or lost in thoughts — while our bodies are neglected. But if you are coming out of a bad relationship, taking care of your physical self is just as important as your emotional wellbeing. And if fact, when your head is a mess, it's sometimes a good idea to go back to basics — food, water, exercise, sleep — as a way of rebuilding your wellbeing.

8.   Give back

What selfish people don't realize is that giving to others can reward the giver just as much as the recipient. Taking the time to offer kindness to others is a way of taking care of yourself — volunteer, spend some time playing with a child, raise some money for a good cause, or help a friend out. You'll feel your own happiness rise along with those you are helping.

9.   Plan for the future

Once you have taken care of the present moment, spend some time making your future brighter. What can you do today that will make you feel better in a year's time? Think of what you would like to do and where you would like to be and reverse-engineer the process by thinking of what you can do now to get there.

Maybe you need to do some further training or look for some freelance work to fund a dream holiday. Maybe you want to be healthier and fitter, so today you need to push yourself to go for a run. Maybe you want to write a book, so today you set aside an hour to write 500 words.

Keeping a big picture to-do list of what you want your life to look like will guide you in your daily choices and keep you focused on your happiness and life goals.

Chapter 7 - Loving Again

So you've begun to recover from your relationship with a narcissist and you're ready to move forward. Or are you? In this chapter, we'll look at dating and how you can avoid making the same mistakes again with your new partner.

We'll also cover some attitude shifts you need to make so you can enjoy better relationships. We've covered red flags to look out for, and in this chapter, we'll go one step further and look at the early signs that show you've found a good partner. Finally, we'll cover good habits to get a new relationship off to a healthy start.

You can set the terms of a relationship to some extent, and the start is the best time to do it. Ideally, you will have spent some time thinking about relationships and your own patterns, and you will be feeling fresh and energized and ready to venture out into the world of dating again.

What can you do to ensure that your new relationships get off to the very best start? Plenty, as it happens. But first of all, let's look at some things you should definitely avoid.

7 Mistakes to Avoid When You Start Dating Again

If you have been in a relationship with a narcissist, you may still be carrying unhelpful beliefs about what a partner should say and do. Your judgment can be skewed by spending time with the wrong people. You may also feel as if your confidence has taken a hit. First of all, there's no need to rush straight back out into dating.

Give yourself as much time as you need to recover, using any or all of the ideas I mentioned in the previous chapter. Always bear in mind that you'll need to tread carefully to avoid making the same mistakes again.

Here are some common pitfalls to look out for when you start dating again.

1. **Hiding the truth of who you are**

In the the world of dating, it can feel that we need to present ourselves as a shiny package, with interesting hobbies, a great body, and a happy, untroubled face. Don't fall into that trap. Be honest about who you are with everyone you meet, don't feel you have to please or impress, and you will find that the right people come to you.

What if you read this and think — but I don't know who I am? Get curious. Get to know and feel comfortable with yourself, either on your own or with the guidance of a therapist, so when you step out into the world you'll feel more certain of what you're about and less likely to be unsettled by a narcissist.

2. **Rushing in too quickly**

As we've seen already, narcissists are adept at moving fast at the start of a new relationship, only for it to fall apart fairly quickly once the initial buzz wears off. Be aware of this tendency when you meet someone and look out for love bombing. Most importantly, take it slow. Don't get drunk and go home with your date that first night, and definitely don't share all your secrets.

Take any outrageous love bombing or commitment talk with a large pinch of salt. If it's meant to be, taking your time won't make a difference. On this note, and it has to be said, don't sleep with someone on the first date if you are thinking it might be a longer-term relationship.

3. Expecting them to commit exclusively

As above, take things slowly. Dating is all about getting to know people, and you can't expect someone to commit just to you on a first date, or even second or third. If someone seems ready to sweep you away and is already talking about an exclusive relationship after three hours in your company, don't fall for it! Someone who falls into infatuation this fast is likely to fall out of it just as quickly, and you are the one who will get burned.

4. Forgetting to enjoy yourself

It's easy to feel like it's all destined to fail after a bad relationship. If you are feeling cynical and bitter, it might be that you're not yet ready or you just haven't found the right person.

You had a bad experience, and that can put you off the whole world of dating in the same way that a bout of food poisoning can put your off the particular food for life. But remember, dating can also be fun. There are — believe it or not — lots of decent, kind, caring people out there who just want to meet someone themselves to spend time with.

You had some bad luck. But it's not your destiny. With some self-care and time to reflect, you will have done some important personal growth that will stand you in good stead when you are ready to try again. Try not to take it too seriously and remember the benefits of mindfulness and gratitude as you move forward. Life is there to be enjoyed, otherwise, what's the point?

An important disclaimer: if you really aren't enjoying life or you feel genuinely anxious and depressed, all the uplifting messages, mindfulness and gratitude in the world might not be enough to make you feel better. Always, always reach out and seek help if you are struggling. See your GP, talk to someone.

5. Seeing a partner as the be-all and end all

You can be perfectly happy single. Oddly, for many people, it's only when they are truly happy on their own and not looking to meet anyone that they actually find someone to commit to.

If you feel that finding someone is an urgent priority in your life, you need to step back a little. Find ways of enjoying time on your own. Spend a whole day on your own doing things you enjoy, make friends with yourself and give yourself the kind of company you would enjoy from someone else.

If you really do feel that finding someone is a matter of urgency, you will only make things harder for yourself. New relationships thrive best in an atmosphere of ease and unhurried fun.

6. Not keeping an open mind

If you have an idea of what your new partner should be like and it's absolutely set in stone, you're going to run into problems. That ideal partner might not exist. Or the ideal partner for you might be nothing like the one you have in your head. My advice is to keep an open mind in general, not just with dating. Be flexible and try new experiences (while always maintaining safe boundaries and looking after yourself).

7. Not trusting your gut

This is probably the most important thing you can do to avoid repeating the same mistake with a relationship. Sure, you might really like someone. They might be attractive, funny, charming and seem to be really into you. It all looks wonderful on the surface as they say and do all the right things.

But how does it feel?

As humans, we are wired to pick up on all sorts of non-verbal signals when interacting with others to work out if they are safe or not. We aren't aware of them a lot of the time, so we can get into the habit of overriding or ignoring these messages from our unconscious if they don't fit in with what we think we want — a relationship, someone to go out with, marriage, babies...
But listening to, and trusting your gut — and then responding to what it is telling you — is one of the smartest things you can do for both your physical and emotional safety.

It may mean being rude and leaving a date or not going home with someone who is incredibly charming and persuasive. It may mean getting told you're rude or difficult.

Don't worry. If you are with someone, and your gut feels tense, or you feel a general sense of uneasiness that you can't quite shake off, believe those messages, and get away as quickly as you can.

If there is one message I hope you will take away from this book, it's this: ***Always trust your gut.***

5 Early Signs You've Finally Found a Good Partner

Now that we've discovered what not to do when we start dating again, let's move onto the good stuff: finding someone who is going to make your world a happier place, not turn it upside down. There are many signs you can look out for that will show you you're on the right track with a new partner.

Here are some things to look out for when you start dating that will signal you've found someone you are compatible with.

1. You feel physically at ease in their presence

If you're with someone who is good for you, who isn't going to harm you, you will probably get a warm and easy feeling. The conversation will flow smoothly most of the time. You won't find yourself worrying about what you've said or done, and you will be enjoying yourself.

You'll feel physically safe, comfortable and relaxed. Look for those feelings when you start dating and believe in them, even if the person isn't necessarily your dream partner in every way — sometimes it happens that way.

2. You share common interests and concerns

No matter how attractive someone is or how charming, in a long-term relationship, there needs to be more than just chemistry. If you feel that you share some similar interests and passions, it's a great sign of compatibility. This does not mean someone who agrees with everything you say. It's more about sounding out your world view and knowing pretty quickly that the other person in on the same page.

This isn't to say that you need to be compatible in all ways. In fact, it's great to have some areas where you have absolutely nothing in common. Someone with different interests can teach you about things you've never found interesting before. On the other hand, having interests that your partner doesn't share gives you a sense of space and allows you to maintain a separate identity.

Keep in mind that it's good to enjoy time off in the same way. If you love traveling and your prospective partner does not own a passport, a lifelong relationship may not be in the cards. If they are hugely invested in a hobby — cycling, gaming, running — that doesn't interest you at all, you might need to manage your expectations about their availability.

But if you find that you enjoy at least some of the same things — even if it's as simple as cuddling up on the couch together watching old movies — then chances are you'll enjoy each other's company.

3. They turn up when they say they will

Narcissists are great at running late, creating drama with last-minute cancellations and let-downs. They make a great deal of fuss around the simple act of gracing you with their presence. It's not surprising that being around them can feel hectic and stressful.

What does the opposite experience look like? If someone just shows up on time, looking friendly and relaxed, and you have a nice time together — talking, chatting, walking, seeing a movie or just enjoying a coffee together — you can start to let down your guard and relax.

When you start seeing someone, it should feel like getting to know a friend or work colleague more than a scene straight out of a Hollywood movie. It should feel relaxed, easy, fun. You should feel curious and enlivened, not overwhelmed or swamped with emotion and chemistry. There should be some chemistry, yes, but it shouldn't feel too urgent or over-the-top.

4. They are consistently kind and interested in you

Remember when we looked at intermittent reinforcement? The opposite of this is consistency. If someone is nice to you, but only sometimes, my advice would be to back off. But if someone is consistently pleasant and kind — not over the top, just decent — then you may well be in the presence of a keeper.

Don't waste your time on someone who is only available sometimes, or who gives you just the crumbs of their attention. Generally, if someone likes you, **you know it**. It's not a mystery. If you find yourself wondering about where you stand with someone, it's likely that you aren't their top priority.

5. You share similar lifestyles

Sleep, food, exercise, levels of tidiness and daily habits such as reading or exercising — all of these mundane things make up the way you live your life. If you see some compatibility in the small things, then that is a very good sign for your future together. If you walk into someone's house and like the way it looks and feels (rather than feeling impressed, awed, or just slightly nonplussed), you should trust that feeling. A long-term relationship isn't about mindblowing passion and chemistry. It's about enjoying your daily life together, and your daily habits are a big part of this.

On this note, if you want to make your life easier, pay attention to how someone presents themselves and their living space. If they appear uncared for or chaotic, that should give you pause. And if that person is dependent on alcohol or other substances, be aware that they may not have the resources to be a good partner.

8 Great Habits to Start Your New Relationship the Right Way
1. Slow and steady

Hold back when you meet someone new. Remember, if they are the one you have all the time in the world to enjoy that fact. If they are not, you should enjoy the relationship for what it is, but also protect yourself so you don't find yourself having to heal and recover from a disastrous relationship.

2. Treat them as you would like to be treated

Set the tone for the relationship you would like to have with someone by being that person yourself. Be kind. Be on time. Communicate as clearly as you can. A new relationship is a fresh start, and you can steer it in the right direction by being respectful and positive.

Even when arguments come along — and they will — remember that you have something special between you and you need to look after that, even if you are having a temporary disagreement. It's possible to fight with someone while still remaining respectful and not doing any permanent damage to the bond between you.

If it's meant to be, you'll have set the groundwork for a rich and loving relationship by treating your partner as you would like to be treated.

3. Focus on the other person

To build a strong relationship takes time and effort. It's often the result of many daily interactions, and learning to focus on someone and respond to them is a useful skill for any relationship, not just a romantic one.

To do this, first of all, eliminate distractions. Make time to spend with your partner, switch off screens, listen and focus. Even if you are busy and rushing off in separate directions, eye contact and affection can go a long way in maintaining a healthy and loving connection into the future.

4. Look after yourself

Just because you've met someone new, this doesn't give you an excuse to stop your efforts to heal from your experience with a narcissist. Keep doing all those things you did to recover — talking to a therapist, looking after your physical and mental wellbeing, journaling and spending time alone to rest and recharge. Taking time out to reflect on where the relationship is going and how you are feeling is another way of looking after yourself as you move forward.

Even in the early days, get in the habit of setting aside some personal space, even if you feel like being with them all the time. Give them time to miss you and feel curious about what you've been up to. It's important to give yourself time to enjoy your own company.

5. Don't dwell in the past

Whatever happened with the narcissist, don't let yourself dwell too much on it if it makes you feel bad. Of course, you need to spend some time on it, either alone or with a therapist, but don't live there. When you find yourself ruminating or wondering how the narcissist is going, bring yourself firmly back into the present with self-care or distraction.

On this note, don't assume that all of your future partners are going to let you down. If you have done some work on yourself and reflected on what may have led you to your narcissistic partner, you should be able to avoid carrying this baggage into your new relationship. Give this new person a chance.

6. Remind yourself of how far you have come

If you have been in a relationship with a narcissist, you've been through quite an experience. Always remind yourself of the fact that you got yourself away, you are now safe, and you have a lot to look forward to.

If you find yourself regretting the time you spent with them, remind yourself that you have a whole future ahead of you that they no longer have the power to ruin. You are safe. You deserve to be happy.

7. Don't badmouth the relationship to others

If you are starting out with someone, it's sometimes a good idea to let it grow in its own time, and in private, before you start talking about it too much to others. It's natural to want to share your new relationship with friends, but just be mindful of how much you share. Try to keep some things private. There are a couple of reasons for this.

First, letting others into your new world with this person too quickly, particularly if they prefer you single, can have a negative impact on the new relationship. Secondly, talking about the relationship in detail with others has a way of taking away energy from its growth and opening up the new bond you have formed to the influence of others, who may not have your best interests at heart.

If you aren't sure about how it's going but generally feel OK, talk to your new partner, or your journal, or your therapist. And if you feel suddenly upset, don't go rushing off to badmouth your new partner to your friends. A new relationship is a fragile thing, like a seedling or tiny baby, and you need to treat it will care as it grows stronger.

8. Laugh together

Sharing humor is one of the best ways to relieve stress and bond with your partner. And it's what makes being in a relationship with someone so much fun. So don't forget to laugh, enjoy each other's company, and be silly together.

A final word on finding new love

As you move on from the narcissist, remember to be positive and hopeful for the future, but also realistic. Unfortunately, there are some people out there you need to steer well clear of for your own wellbeing and happiness. But there are also many others who will enrich your life. Ultimately, it's about finding that sweet spot between keeping yourself safe and trusting in those that you meet to do the right thing by you.

If the relationship you've had with a narcissist is good for anything, it's that you have learned how to look after yourself in all sorts of new ways. Believe in your new insights, get out there, and have fun!

Conclusion

Hopefully, in this book, you've found out more about yourself and other people. Use this knowledge to enjoy healthy, satisfying, and joyful relationships. We've been on a journey together, and my sincere wish is that you are feeling energized, educated, and ready to face the future.

Let's take a moment to go over the key points of this book.

First, we looked at the reasons for picking it up in the first place: you suspect you may be in a relationship with a narcissist, and you want to find out more. Or you've come out of a bad relationship and you are now wondering — what happened? You may also want to avoid making the same mistakes again or prevent others from doing so.

I firmly believe that you should know your enemy. And getting to know the narcissist and what makes him or her tick is a tool that will stand you in good stead as you move through life.

We also looked at the key traits of narcissists that make them so easy to spot: primarily, a grandiose sense of self, an unshakeable belief that they are special and uniquely talented. They also have a shameless ability to exploit people, abuse others, and put themselves first.

We also looked at what makes someone a narcissist and how a childhood that combines excessive spoiling with periods of neglect is often what sows the seeds of a narcissistic personality disorder. We saw that despite the strong and overpowering way they present themselves, it's actually very lonely inside the narcissist's head, and they aren't nearly as powerful as they need you to think they are.

We discovered the key warning signs of narcissists, and some of their most common tactics, including gaslighting, love bombing, intermittent reinforcement, and narcissistic rage. The manipulative tactics of narcissists can be quite unsettling to those who are used to more straightforward communication, but once you know and understand them, you are better equipped to deal with them. And most importantly, you've stopped wondering if it's all in your head.

You now know many of the telling phrases that narcissists come out with and what triggers them. You can identify the kinds of people they are attracted to — usually kind and empathic souls who tend to give others the benefit of the doubt. We also looked at how to avoid triggering the narcissist and feeling the full fury of one of their attacks.

Simply put, you can't reason with a narcissist and you can't expect the same reasonable responses from them that you would get from others. Being around a narcissist is not like being around most people — what you need to focus on is primarily protecting yourself, and also managing them so that they can keep themselves under control.

An important point we touched on here is that the narcissist can't change. There is nothing you can do that will improve their behavior, and accepting this and moving forward as best you can is the only sane response.

We then moved on to how this affects their victims. We looked at the damage it can do to you, and why you must leave or disengage for your own wellbeing. Narcissists are very good at manipulating their victims, at holding on tightly when they show signs of leaving and at making a clean break as difficult as possible.

But once you are aware of this, and can keep in mind your own future mental health and wellbeing, you will find within yourself the power to cut the cord for good. The sad thing here is accepting that the narcissist isn't really capable of love or caring relationships, and you need to give up on the hope that you will ever receive what you need from them.

The second part of the book was more active and required more input from you, with lots of techniques and strategies to move forward in your new life, free from this troubling personality.

We looked at how to leave, and the Gray Rock Method as a way of making the narcissist lose interest in you.

We then looked at healing — how to get yourself back to neutral after this disturbing experience, and from there, how to re-energize yourself and move forward with courage, strong self-esteem, and hope.

You discovered all kinds of ways to make yourself stronger and healthier, so that the narcissist can't find a way back in. Mental health options include therapy, meditation, self-love, mantras, and journaling. You can strengthen yourself physically with food, sleep, and exercise. There are so many ways to heal yourself, and I hope you find ones that work for you and enjoy the numerous benefits.

Finally, we looked at breaking the cycle so you don't find yourself in this situation again. We covered what to look for in a relationship, early warning signs, and the signals that you are on the right track to a healthier and more satisfying future.

You deserve to be treated well, you deserve a loving relationship, and I honestly believe that if you do the growth work and take care of yourself, you can find it. Sometimes, a book isn't enough and you need some real-life guidance too: I hope you have the resources and courage to explore further with a trained and compatible therapist, should you need to.

I hope you have enjoyed the journey and found it useful. Narcissists are incredibly frustrating to deal with, and they can do a lot of damage. I wish it weren't the case, but chances are, even if you never have a close relationship with one, you will come across them in your life, your work and your day to day dealings with the world.

Sometimes, you can't simply ignore them. They are widely acknowledged by psychologists as some of the hardest people to treat, so taking the time to read up on them and learn more is a good use of your time and energy. Human nature is fascinating, and you may even get to the point where you can simply enjoy the quirks of a narcissist in your family or working life without being too affected by them.

You now have a whole bunch of effective strategies to deal with narcissists that you can put in place and use as often as you need to (hopefully not at all, but you can't guarantee that!) You know how to look after yourself, how to back away, and how to form healthier and more satisfying relationships with those that will appreciate your presence, time and energy. You know that even if narcissists make it hard for you to leave, you still have the right to do so.

If there is one thing I would like you to take away from this book, it's to **trust your instincts and do whatever you need to to keep safe and happy**. There is no need to suffer with those who aren't good for you, and to give them your time and energy that could be better spent elsewhere.

Narcissists truly are vampires that walk among us, feeding on the good energy of others and at ease with exploiting your kindness and generosity. Don't feel bad about moving away from them, however much they cry and wail. Say no, protect your boundaries, put yourself and your own wellbeing first. You deserve so much more than that from your relationships — and you can have it.